Animals and Misanthropy

This engaging volume explores and defends the claim that misanthropy is a justified attitude towards humankind in the light of how human beings both compare with and treat animals. Reflection on differences between humans and animals helps to confirm the misanthropic verdict, while reflection on the moral and other failings manifest in our treatment of animals illuminates what is wrong with this treatment. Human failings, it is argued, are too entrenched to permit optimism about the future of animals, but ways are proposed in which individual people may accommodate to the truth of misanthropy through cultivating mindful, humble and compassionate relationships to animals. Drawing on both Eastern and Western philosophical traditions David E. Cooper offers an original and challenging approach to the complex field of animal ethics.

David E. Cooper is Emeritus Professor of Philosophy at Durham University, UK. He has been a Visiting Professor at universities in several countries, including the USA and Sri Lanka. His many books include *The Measure of Things: Humanism, Humility and Mystery*, *A Philosophy of Gardens*, *Convergence with Nature: A Daoist Perspective* and *Senses of Mystery: Engaging with Nature and the Meaning of Life*.

PRAISE FOR THIS BOOK

'David E. Cooper's *Animals and Misanthropy* is a meditation on animals and humans. It is also an argument for a negative view of humankind. Humanity's vices, Professor Cooper argues, are in full display in its treatment of animals – beings that are themselves innocent. He writes with sensitivity about animals and without rancour about humans, thus defending a gentle but uncompromising misanthropy. You do not have to be respectful of animals or misanthropic to start reading this book, but don't be surprised if you are both after you have finished it.'

David Benatar, *University of Cape Town, South Africa*

'In this short, powerful book, David E. Cooper argues that honest reflection on the awful situation of animals justifies a charge of misanthropy – a negative moral judgment on human life at large. Surveying practices and institutions such as animal agriculture, we find a variety of human vices and failings – cruelty, insensitivity, hubris – so entrenched and extensive that they warrant critical judgment on nothing less than our way of life itself. By contrast, lucid appreciation of the lives of animals shows them to be characterised by spontaneity and other virtues, alongside a fundamental vulnerability ruthlessly exploited by human beings. By drawing upon the writings of Western and Asian philosophers and others engaged personally and professionally with animals, Cooper advances a charge of misanthropy that corrects vainglorious moral optimism and points to other, better ways to live with animals.'

Ian James Kidd, *University of Nottingham, UK*

'In this lucid and elegant book Cooper draws effortlessly on literature and world philosophy to gather evidence for a bleakly compelling verdict on the morally barbarous condition of humanity through a consideration of how we compare with and treat animals, particularly those at our mercy, refreshing the meaning of misanthropy.'

Michael McGhee, *University of Liverpool, UK*

'*Animals and Misanthropy* explores our dark side as human beings by contrasting it with the innocence of the animals we so often mistreat. It is an important and strikingly original contribution to the field of animal ethics, and essential reading, surely, for anyone concerned with our moral relations to the more-than-human world.'

Simon P. James, *Durham University, UK*

David E.
Cooper

Animals and Misanthropy

Routledge
Taylor & Francis Group

LONDON AND NEW YORK

First published 2018
by Routledge
2 Park Square, Milton Park, Abingdon, Oxon OX14 4RN

and by Routledge
711 Third Avenue, New York, NY 10017

Routledge is an imprint of the Taylor & Francis Group, an informa business

British Library Cataloguing-in-Publication Data
A catalogue record for this book is available from the British Library

Library of Congress Cataloging-in-Publication Data
A catalog record for this title has been requested

ISBN: 978-1-138-29593-3 (hbk)
ISBN: 978-1-138-29594-0 (pbk)
ISBN: 978-1-315-09966-8 (ebk)

Typeset in Joanna MT
by Apex CoVantage, LLC

CONTENTS

Acknowledgements

I am grateful to Simon P. James and Ian James Kidd for their encouraging and useful comments on draft chapters of this book. My thanks go as well to the editorial team at Routledge – Gabrielle Coakeley, Rebecca Shillabeer and Ruth Berry – and to the project manager, Autumn Spalding. It has been a pleasure working with them.

ACKNOWLEDGMENTS

1

MISANTHROPY

PROLOGUE

Some months ago I was walking in the Cheviot hills of Northumberland, enjoying the heather, the gorse, the tumbling streams, and also the singing of birds, the scurrying of rabbits and the glimpse of a fox returning to its den. Even before I turned the bend on the track I was following, I knew my enjoyment was over, for I could hear ahead of me the merry shouting of a party of shooters as they were disgorged from their range rovers. I walked past these men while they collected their guns and game bags from the back of their vehicles.

I disliked these men, for what they were about to do to the pheasants or grouse that would soon be driven towards their guns, but also for how, to me, they looked, sounded and smelt – intoxicated, mindless, vulgar, swaggering and harsh.

My likes and dislikes, of course, are neither here nor there. More interesting, though, is a set of reflections that an encounter like mine in the Cheviots can inspire – reflections that could equally be prompted by, say, footage of an abattoir worker laughing as he clubs a pig to death, or of a laboratory assistant immune to the screams of the dogs to whom she periodically administers electric shocks.

The reflections my encounter prompted were on how relationships between human beings and animals should inform an assessment, an appraisal, of the human condition. By relationships, here, I don't simply mean human attitudes towards and treatment of animals, but also our kinship (or lack of it) to animals, our similarities and dissimilarities to them. Someone who reflects on these matters may come to agree with Friedrich Nietzsche's remark that not only does 'man represent no progress over the animal' but that he has become 'decadent'.[1] Or be inclined to endorse Milan Kundera's judgement that in its 'attitude towards those who are at its mercy' – animals – 'mankind has suffered a fundamental debacle'.[2]

To sympathise with such judgements is to be on the way, at least, to adopting a misanthropic attitude towards humankind. Reflections on our relationships to animals have the power, it seems, to reinforce or even inspire a dark vision and hostile appraisal of our species. There is really no need here for the words 'it seems', since it is clear that the negative assessments of the human condition made by many thinkers have indeed been strengthened by their perceptions of how people compare with or treat animals. Among these thinkers are Zhuangzi and Plutarch in the ancient world and, more recently, Michel de Montaigne, Jean-Jacques Rousseau, Arthur Schopenhauer and Walt Whitman. A contemporary instance is a 2008 book by a philosopher that describes his life with a pet wolf, Brenin. The author, Mark Rowlands, calls himself a 'natural misanthrope', someone who needs to 'tune out human beings'. This need is due, not simply to recognising 'the human evil' manifested in people's treatment of animals, but to appreciation as well of the freedom of wolves and other animals from the vices and failings that contaminate human life – cruelty, deception, ingratitude and the rest.[3]

I want to explore and defend the thought that reflections on our relationships to animals confirm a misanthropic view of humankind. Before I can embark on this, however, there are preliminary issues it is necessary to address. Not least of these, is the matter of how misanthropy should be understood.

FEELINGS AND JUDGEMENTS

Alceste, the eponymous protagonist of Molière's play The Misanthrope, declares that he 'detests all men'.[4] His succinct statement seems to confirm the familiar image of a misanthrope as someone who feels a certain way towards human beings: he or she hates, despises, detests or at the very least dislikes them. But Alceste did not just wake up one morning to find he had an aversion towards his species in the way he might have done to find that he now had an aversion to truffles. His hatred, rather, grew from his perception of his fellow men as 'wicked and evil'. He becomes 'melancholy and grieved' because he 'sees men behave as they do'.

The distinction, within misanthropy, between feelings and judgements was made explicit by Immanuel Kant. While he finds 'contemptible' a feeling of 'anthrophobia', he is able to respect 'a misanthropy . . . in many right-minded men, that . . . [is] the result of long and sad experience' of, amongst much else, the 'falsehood, ingratitude, injustice [and] puerility' that motivate 'all imaginable evils'.[5] For Kant, this latter kind of misanthropy – though he is reluctant to call it that – is a form of appraisal, a recognition of what he elsewhere called 'the crooked timber of humanity'. Later philosophers have followed Kant: the misanthropy they defend or attack is not a feeling of hatred, but a verdict or judgement on humankind.

That said, it would be wrong to compartmentalise feeling and judgement. For one thing, feelings can influence, as well as arise from, judgements. Alceste's melancholy was a response to everywhere finding 'flattery, injustice and roguery', but it then served to intensify his perception of 'this bitter world'. Second, it is often artificial to split a denunciation into two components, feeling and judgement. Charles Baudelaire experienced 'a shudder' when reading in his newspaper about the 'universal atrocity' of human life, but the terms in which he condemns this life – 'loathsome', 'disgusting' – are ones that both register judgement and convey emotion.[6]

Philosophical misanthropes may well entertain feelings of gloom, anger, scorn or hatred, but their mission is to articulate and defend an appraisal of humankind, not to work themselves up into lather of emotion. Their model might be the Buddha. Despite its contemporary smiley image, Buddhism offers a bleak vision of human existence. 'Monks', the Buddha tells his followers, 'all is burning . . . with fire of lust . . . hatred . . . delusion . . . with sorrow, dejection, and despair'.[7] But Gautama himself was not a firebrand preacher: instead, he was coolly, even drily, analytical in his diagnosis of universal suffering as the product of people's own craving and ignorance.

So, misanthropy is to be understood in terms of a certain kind of judgement or appraisal. But what kind? How close, for example, is misanthropy to 'the wisdom of Silenus'? When King Midas pressed the god of wine, Dionysus's companion, Silenus, to identify 'the most desirable thing among mankind', the reply came: 'the best is not to be born at all', and the next best 'to die as soon as we can'.[8] (Despite the association with Silenus, similar ancient proclamations are found in *Ecclesiastes* 4.3 and in Sophocles's drama, *Oedipus at Colonus*.) A modern descendant of Silenus's wisdom is the doctrine of anti-natalism.[9] Better that human beings had never been at all, but given that they are, the next best thing is to ensure, by ceasing to procreate, that they will not be around in the future.

Misanthropes, even of the darkest hue, are not however committed to anti-natalism. That it would have been better if people had never drunk alcohol does not mean that, now that they do, prohibition is the best policy. Humankind is up and running, and even if this is regrettable, it is not self-evident that bringing its existence to an end is obligatory. Maybe the more advisable course is to make the best of a bad job, or to devote our energies to amelioration of the human condition. The Silenian or anti-natalist verdict should perhaps be regarded, not as equivalent to the misanthropic judgement, but as a dramatic, rhetorical way of voicing an especially intense version of misanthropy.

And how close, we can also ask, is misanthropy to another '-ism' with which it is often associated: pessimism? The term was introduced in the eighteenth century as an antonym to 'optimism', the name Leibniz gave to his doctrine that our world, since it is the creation of a perfect God, is the best of all possible worlds. (If it wasn't, then its Maker would not, after all, be perfect.) The term has, of course, altered in sense but, in philosophical literature at least, it remains the name of a negative judgement rather than, as in everyday talk, of a gloomy or despondent feeling.[10] Schopenhauer, for example, is counted as a pessimist not because he felt depressed or hopeless but because he saw human life as oscillating between frustration and boredom. It was Eduard von Hartmann's conclusion that happiness is impossible, not his personal disposition and moods, that made him a celebrated philosophical pessimist in the nineteenth century.

The pessimist, then, joins the misanthropist in a negative assessment of the human condition, but their respective emphases are different. The pessimist's focus is on aspects of this condition – suffering, frustration, absurdity – that are destructive of the possibility of happiness and fulfilment. The misanthrope's concern, by contrast, is with human failings, ingredients of life for which humankind is answerable and rightly held to account. For the pessimist, it is at least imaginable that universal suffering and unhappiness are, as it were, bad luck and due to nothing for which human beings are themselves responsible.

The contrast should not be overdone, however, for pessimism and misanthropy are typically found in harness. Schopenhauer, for example, inherited from the Buddha a pessimistic view of the world as an arena of suffering. But he explains that this 'melancholy' translates into misanthropy with the recognition that the human world is 'a den of thieves', a place of 'boundless egoism' and 'moral depravity'.[11] As this suggests, pessimism and misanthropy are not simply conjoined, but serve to reinforce one another. The vices exposed by the misanthrope – Schopenhauer's list includes 'greed, gluttony, lust, self-interest, avarice, hard-heartedness. . . [and] arrogance' – help to explain the scale of the miseries attended to by the pessimist. Conversely, it is people's unhappiness, frustration and boredom that fuels their 'moral depravity', meanness of spirit or gluttony.

So, pessimism and misanthropy typically endorse one another. But there is inflection here, as well. At any rate, a form of pessimism that is not informed by misanthropy is liable to seem shallow. The horror stories writer, Thomas Ligotti, is unusual in wanting to keep them entirely apart, holding that 'man's inhumanity to man' is irrelevant to the author's own pessimistic denial that '[b]eing alive is alright'.[12] But this makes one wonder what he thinks a life that is 'alright' might be like. Not a life, it seems, that includes kindness, respect or charity. On a more orthodox understanding of a good life, these virtues do not simply contribute to happiness and fulfilment but are ingredients of them. Similarly, the suffering on which pessimists focus does not consist solely in the pain and distress that our failings result in: rather, as the Buddha emphasised, it is partly constituted by those failings, by our 'taints' and 'cankers'. People consumed by hate, envy or greed are not happy or fulfilled: their lives are ones of *dukkha* – 'suffering', 'unsatisfactoriness'. Or, as a contemporary author, Alain de Botton, observes, the 'frailty and fragility' of our lives to which a 'pessimistic realist' attends are not intelligible in isolation from the jealousy, infidelity and other failings that infect these lives.[13] The jealous person, for instance, is always at risk, her fragile happiness dependent on the uncertain affections and loyalties of other people.

Misanthropy, then, is a critical judgement on human life, infused as it is by failings that are ubiquitous, pronounced and entrenched. But what failings? A tempting answer is that misanthropy is an exposé of our *moral* failings. Alceste's misanthropy, after all, seemed to consist in a recognition that human beings are 'wicked and evil'. But the term 'moral', even on a fairly expansive understanding of it, is too narrow to encompass all the failings on which the misanthrope's case depends. In a famously misanthropic novel inspired by his experiences of the army, hospitals and slums, Louis-Ferdinand Céline calls his fellow men 'devilish', but he also calls them 'obscene', 'putrescent' and 'packages of rotten tripe' – words that register more an aesthetic than a moral revulsion.[14] 'Moral' becomes still narrower in its compass when understood as it tends to be in contemporary Western moral philosophy, where moral concern is identified with concerns for rights, obligations, fairness and individual autonomy. On this understanding, racial prejudice and sexism will be moral failings, but not vulgarity, over-ambition, blindness to beauty, jealousy, gluttony, mindlessness, meanness and vanity.

These, however, were among the many failings that ancient philosophers – Chinese, Greek, Indian – rightly counted as destructive of the good life, as inimical to human flourishing. So, like those philosophers, the misanthrope is speaking not only of moral failings in today's restricted sense, but of many others – of spiritual, aesthetic, intellectual, emotional traits that detract from the good life, from what human existence should be like.

'Failing' is a bland term, too insipid, you may feel, to capture what we find wrong in, say, cruelty and cowardice, or wilful ignorance and self-deception. But I can't think of another term with sufficient scope. 'Vice' – my original choice – is too suggestive of specifically moral culpability. Vices are only one kind of human failing, albeit a kind that will be especially prominent in later chapters. I was also tempted to borrow from the Buddhist arsenal of labels for our failings – 'cankers', 'taints', 'defilements', 'fetters' and so on. But none of these has sufficient generality, and each has a technical sense within Buddhist teachings. Anyway, 'failings' does at least have the advantage of possessing critical force. People may not be to blame for their failures – 'the gods' or Sod's law may be the culprit – but they are always answerable for their failings. So, 'failings' it is, though where appropriate in particular contexts I will use the names of more specific kinds of failing, notably 'vices'. Sometimes, too, I'll talk of 'broadly moral' judgements and failings, with 'broadly' serving to remind the reader that 'moral' is not to be taken in the narrow senses just mentioned.

I take it as evident that most, if not all, of the failings I have mentioned – meanness, cowardice, envy and so on – really are failings. Elaborations and caveats will occasionally become necessary, but in a book that is not a work of general ethics, I feel no obligation to argue at length for something that, I hope, most readers will likewise take as evident.

HUMAN BEINGS, HUMANKIND, HUMAN NATURE

In clarifying misanthropy, it is important to ask who or what is the target – the constituency, one might say – of misanthropic judgements. To whom or to what do the moral and other failings that support these judgements belong? The obvious answer, it might seem, is human beings, individual men and women. This is too simple, however. All human beings? Most? Only some?

When Schopenhauer refers to 'the boundless egoism of everyone, the malice of most, the cruelty of many', he implies that the size of the target varies according to the particular human failing in question.[15] He's clearly right: more of us, I imagine, are prone to jealousy and sentimentality, say, than to vengefulness and emotional frigidity.

Schopenhauer is also right, more interestingly, to suggest elsewhere that, in some contexts, the misanthrope's target is not individual people at all. He viewed human beings as playthings of a cosmic 'will to live' that drives their actions. 'Everyone', he proclaims, 'is nothing but this will'.[16] Because of this, his most scathing judgements are not on individual men and women, but on human existence or human life, through which the blind will that is the essential nature of reality relentlessly courses.

It is not necessary to subscribe to Schopenhauer's metaphysics of the will to accept that the target of misanthropic judgements may be something less concrete than individual people. Humankind, the human way of life or human existence could instead be targets. The important thing is to recognise that a verdict on humankind or human existence is not equivalent to one on individual human beings. This is no more puzzling than the fact that judgements we pass on clubs, armies, industries and other organisations are not equivalent to judgements on the men and women who belong to them. When an army regiment, for example, is criticised for its lack of *esprit de corps*, it may be possible to pick out certain soldiers as especially culpable: but, even if it is, the regiment's failure to meet a standard of military virtue is not reducible to the apathy, cowardice or whatever of these particular men or women. And this is for something like the reason Schopenhauer gave: people may be caught up or immersed in, shaped and constrained by something not of their own making.

What people are caught up in and constrained by need not be anything as grand as Schopenhauer's cosmic will. It could be an ambience or a system, or – at a more general level – a culture, a form of social and economic life, a *Lebenswelt*. One thinks, here, of Martin Heidegger's portrait of everyday life as one in which what individuals do, think and feel is under the 'dictatorship' of 'Them' (*das man*), the anonymous, faceless, pervasive source and shaper of people's opinions, beliefs and hopes.[17] Or of the Daoist, Zhuangzi's, perception – two thousand years earlier – of a human world in which individuals 'all follow the times', their lives 'submerged in the thousand things', victims of a culture and economy that demand constant 'busy-ness', 'accumulation' and mechanical, unreflective routine.[18] It may well be that certain individual participants in a form of life stand out for their viciousness, narcissism or other failings. But the badness of the form of life does not consist in – it is not exhausted by – the failings of these particular people. This is a point, we'll see later, emphasised by critics of several of our worst practices towards animals.

So, while I shall sometimes talk of human beings as the target of the misanthrope's verdict, I shall also refer to humankind, human existence or forms of human life instead. Should there be added to this list human *nature*? Care is needed here, however. The expression 'human nature', to modern ears, is liable to be taken as meaning the biological, genetic make-up of our species. Now, this is what some misanthropes may have in mind. When the landscape designer and environmentalist, Ian McHarg, proclaimed that 'Man is an epidemic . . . a planetary disease' that is killing the planet, he intended an emphasis on human beings as a biological species.[19] But this is not generally the emphasis of misanthropes. For them, as for their critics as well, human beings are not members of a biological kind alone: they are also persons, belonging to a kind, therefore, that could possibly include non-biological beings (ghosts, gods, angels, robots, metallic Martians).[20] The dimensions of human life on which misanthropes focus are not those studied by geneticists or anatomists, but cultural, social, spiritual and moral ones. And the comparisons they make between human and animal existence are not those between biological species.

Even when human nature is not understood in a biological sense, there remains a problem with taking human nature as the target of misanthropy. To do so is to take sides on an issue that has long divided misanthropic thinkers. Jean-Jacques Rousseau asked which of the two, 'natural man' or 'civilised man', was 'wicked', 'coarse and depraved'. His answer was civilised man. Natural man, by contrast, was 'good', 'at peace with all nature', 'the friend of all his fellows'.[21] Rousseau intended his answer to contradict the one given by most earlier political theorists, including Thomas Hobbes, for whom human life in a state of nature, prior to civilisation, was 'nasty and brutish'. The mistake of these thinkers, according to Rousseau, was to attribute to savage people traits they could only have developed in civilised society – in effect, to attribute to human nature what is really the product of human culture.

Rather than side with Rousseau or with Hobbes, the wiser course is to soften the contrast between nature and culture. To begin with, it was hardly unnatural for people to have developed the technologies, languages, arts, codes of behaviour and economic practices that, among much else, constitute a culture or civilisation. Except for people with certain theological commitments, there is no reason to reject an explanation of these developments in Darwinian terms of adaption and selection. Second, it is unclear that human nature in the biologist's sense has not changed through cultural innovations. Human nature in this sense, some argue, is not constant, but has adapted in response to agriculture and domestication – developments that altered what traits were genetically advantageous to people.[22]

It's important to note, next, that the 'savage' or 'natural men' described by Rousseau and other eighteenth-century enthusiasts for the primitive are people whose relation to nature is already, to a degree, culturally shaped. Their ways of eating and dressing, for example, served to satisfy natural needs, but were also subject to conventions and taboos, and used techniques and materials that were the products of complex social cooperation. They didn't, for example, just stuff edible matter into their mouths, but ate meals with family and friends.

Indeed, it is hard to maintain that it is possible, even in principle, to split the practices, perceptions and attitudes of human beings into 'natural' and 'cultural' components. Human life is a set of ways of engaging with the world that cannot be bisected into those that owe to inborn needs and tendencies and those that owe to how people have learned to cope with and communicate about the world. As Maurice Merleau-Ponty put it, 'it is not possible to say that nature begins here and man or expression begins here'.[23]

For these and other reasons, I won't add human nature to the list of the misanthrope's targets – human beings, humankind, human life. None of these reasons, however, require one to deny that, in obvious respects, the lives of people were once – and in some places, still are – 'closer to nature' than those of us living in modern, developed societies. In order to eat, we do not, as they had to, depend on the migrations of animals. In order not to freeze or bake, we do not need, as they did, radically to adjust everyday living according to the season of the year.

Nor should the lack of a clear boundary between the cultural and the natural obstruct a decision to focus, in an appraisal of human failings, upon the life of Rousseau's 'civilised man'. Upon, that is, human life as it has evolved into modern times; upon forms of human life as this is led in the social worlds with which we are familiar. Interesting as it is to speculate on the moral, spiritual and other virtues and failings of our hunter-gatherer ancestors, most of us are more interested in those that we find among ourselves, in forms of life that are, or are close to, the ones in which we participate and collude.

In a book that reflects on how our relationships with animals confirm a misanthropic judgement on humankind, it would be strange for the emphasis not to be upon 'civilised man'. This is because these relationships have been radically transformed through developments in agriculture, domestication, industry, medicine, sport and other practices that constitute what we ordinarily think of as civilisation. For example, the domestication of animals – especially in the form of selective breeding – has not only altered the anatomy and character of many species, brought new kinds of animal, such as breeds of dogs, into being, but also shaped how animals get perceived and treated.[24] That the emphasis is upon modernity is not, of course, to deny the value, at certain points, of comparisons with what we can glean about our hunter-gatherer ancestors. Such comparisons, indeed, will help to render salient aspects of our forms of life.

Misanthropy, in summary, is understood in the chapters that follow, not as hatred or dislike of one's fellow human beings, but as a dark, negative appraisal of human existence. It is a verdict based on a perception of our failings as ubiquitous, pronounced and entrenched – at least in the world of 'civilised man' with which we are familiar and in which we are actors, a world that some see as 'liberating itself from the controlling mechanism of goodness'.[25] I have intentionally left some aspects of misanthropy unspecific, both the target of the misanthrope's verdict and the type of failings exposed. Whether the target is best referred to as humankind, forms of human life, human beings at large or even human nature, will vary according to context. And whether particular failings are best called moral, intellectual, emotional or spiritual will likewise vary. Specificity is not always called for or desirable. Human failings are too plentiful and diffuse to be squeezed under just one or two labels, and the constituencies on which the misanthrope passes judgement do not fall under a single neat heading. None of this prevents our recognising the misanthrope's targets or the failings that are exposed. Nothing, therefore, prevents us from proceeding to ask how our relationships with animals are relevant to the misanthropic appraisal of our existence. It is time, then, to introduce animals into the discussion.

NOTES

1 Friedrich Nietzsche, *The Will to Power*, New York: Vintage, 1968, § 90.

2 Milan Kundera, *The Unbearable Lightness of Being*, London: Faber & Faber, 1985, p. 289.

3 Mark Rowlands, *The Philosopher and the Wolf*, London: Granta, 2008, pp. 21, 146.

4 The following quotes from *The Misanthrope* may all be found at www. goodreads.com/quotes/685838-le-misanthrope-ou-l-atrabilaire-amoureux. Accessed 21/05/2017.

5 Immanuel Kant, *The Critique of Judgement*, Oxford: Oxford University Press, 1952, p. 129.

6 Charles Baudelaire, *Intimate Journals*, San Francisco, CA: City Light Books, 1990, p. 91.

7 *In the Buddha's Words: An Anthology of Discourses from the Pāli Canon*, ed. Bhikkhu Bodhi, Boston: Wisdom Publications, 2005, p. 346.

8 Aristotle, *Eudemus* fragment, https://en.m.wikipedia.org/wiki/Silenus. Accessed 22/05/2017.

9 See David Benatar, *Better Not to Have Been: The Harm of Coming into Existence*, Oxford: Oxford University Press, 2006.

10 See Joshua Foa Dienstag, *Pessimism: Philosophy, Ethic, Spirit*, Princeton, NJ: Princeton University Press, 2006.

11 Arthur Schopenhauer, *The Two Fundamental Problems of Ethics*, Oxford: Oxford University Press, 2010, pp. 200, 210.

12 Thomas Ligotti, *The Conspiracy against the Human Race: The Continuance of Horror*, New York: Hippocampus, 2010, p. 191.

13 Alain de Botton, in *Do Humankind's Best Days Lie Ahead?: Munk Debate 2015*, London: OneWorld, 2016, pp. 14, 71.

14 Louis-Ferdinand Céline, *Journey to the End of the Night*, London: Penguin, 1966, pp. 22, 292, 361, 368.

15 Schopenhauer, *The Two Fundamental Problems of Ethics*, p. 200.

16 Schopenhauer, *The World as Will and Representation*, Vol. 1, New York: Dover, 1969, p. 397.

17 Martin Heidegger, *Being and Time*, Oxford: Blackwell, 1980, § 27.

18 In Eske Møllgaard, *An Introduction to Daoist Thought: Action, Language and Ethics in Zhuangzi*, London: Routledge, 2007, pp. 17–19.

19 Ian McHarg, *Man: The Planetary Disease*, B.Y. Morrison Memorial Lecture, Washington, DC: Agriculture Research Service, pp. 1–2.

20 See Roger Scruton, *On Human Nature*, Princeton, NJ: Princeton University Press, 2017, especially pp. 19, 45, 48.

21 Jean-Jacques Rousseau, *Discourse on the Origin of Inequality*, Oxford: Oxford University Press, 1994, pp. 94–7.

22 For discussions of this issue, see Carl Safina, *Beyond Words: What Animals Think*, London: Souvenir, 2015, p. 235, and Steven Pinker, *The Better Angels of Our Nature*, London: Penguin, 2011, pp. 739ff.

23 Maurice Merleau-Ponty, 'Eye and Mind', in T. Baldwin (ed.), *Maurice Merleau-Ponty: Basic Writings*, London: Routledge, 2004, p. 319.

24 On the effects of domestication, see Jim Mason, *An Unnatural Order: The Roots of Our Destruction of Nature*, New York: Lantern, 1993, Chapter 4, and Safina, *Beyond Words*, pp. 221–39.

25 Lazlo Krasznahorkai, *The Last Wolf*, London: Tuskar Rock, 2016, p. 117.

2

INTRODUCING ANIMALS

Why animals? Why, that is, may discussion of animals and their connections with human beings bear upon, and indeed confirm, a misanthropic judgement on humankind? For two reasons, both of which I mentioned at the beginning and that I will elaborate in this chapter. But, first, I want to put aside an association between animals and misanthropy that people often allege.

A FALSE START

There are some surprisingly popular claims that share the idea that compassionate concern for animals is a symptom of misanthropy. In one especially cynical version, the thought is that such concern is typically disingenuous, a disguise for a person's antipathy to human beings. This is the thrust of Lord Macaulay's quip that 'the Puritan hated bearbaiting, not because it gave pain to the bear, but because it gave pleasure to the spectators'. The same thought is also by voiced by defenders of fox hunting who accuse their urban opponents of feeling, not sympathy for the foxes, but antipathy to the countrified gentry they imagine to be the main aficionados of hunting. Macaulay himself, though, didn't suppose that all campaigners for animals, including his contemporaries who 'interfer[ed] for the purpose of protecting beasts against the wanton cruelty of man', were faking their compassion.[1] Nor, of course, is every critic of fox hunting motivated by class prejudice. Like most cynical charges, this one generalises from what is at best true of some people. 'At best', since one wonders if any aficionado of hunting really believes that class hatred is the sole, or even the main, cause of opposition to blood sports.

Taken in the spirit it was intended, Macaulay's quip about the Puritans, it's been said, 'captures the insight that zoophily can shade into misanthropy'.[2] Perhaps what is meant by this is that many people who devote energy to the welfare of animals do so not only out of compassion for animals, but because they lack compassion for human beings. A related idea is that many pet lovers are people who are unable to experience companionship with and affection for their fellow humans.

It is true that some misanthropic authors combine zoophily with marked antipathy to human beings. Good examples are those two great lovers of raptors, the American poet Robinson Jeffers and the English author of The Peregrine, J.A. Baker. Were it not for the penalties, Jeffers tells us, he would 'sooner kill a man than a hawk'.[3] Baker, who increasingly identified with the falcon he followed each day for a year, shared the bird's 'hatred of the sound of man, that faceless horror of the stony places'.[4] But it would be as wrong to generalise from these instances as it was from the Puritan hatred of bear-baiting enthusiasts and the town-dweller's dislike of country gentlemen hunters.

Two wider replies can be made to the charge that concern for animals is symptomatic of misanthropy. To begin with, it seems to rest on a quaint conception of compassion or sympathy as something that is found, in the human heart, in a fixed quantity.

As Mary Midgley puts it, compassion is being 'treated hydraulically', like a 'fluid'.[5] If expended on animals, none is left over for human beings – like the water in a can that is poured over the dahlias, leaving nothing for the hydrangeas. Contrary to this image, however, we know that many leading champions of animal welfare – including Voltaire and J.S. Mill – also campaigned against poverty and other human ills. The evidence also shows that people who contribute to animal charities are more, not less likely, to contribute as well to medical and overseas famine charities. And we know, too, that people who treat their fellows cruelly are the ones most likely to treat animals, including their unfortunate pets, in the same way.

The second objection is that those who regard compassion for animals as a symptom of misanthropy are construing misanthropy as a feeling, as hatred or dislike of human beings. But this, as explained in Chapter 1, is not what we are understanding by misanthropy. Instead, it is a kind of judgement or assessment of humankind. Even if it were true, then, that warmth of feeling towards animals is associated with emotional coldness towards people, the point would be irrelevant. The misanthrope is not hard of heart, but harsh in judgement. As we'll shortly see, the hawk-loving pair, Jeffers and Baker, display their misanthropy, in the relevant sense, not through their sour remarks on their fellows, but through their bleak assessment of human attitudes and behaviour.

So, it is not through an imagined association between attitudes to animals and dislike of human beings that our relations to animals are relevant to misanthropy. Let's turn to the relations that are relevant.

TWO KINDS OF REFLECTION

That there are two very different types of relations to animals that are germane to the topic of misanthropy was briefly indicated at the start of the book. One type consists in similarities and differences between humans and animals, the other in our treatment of and attitudes towards animals. To elaborate on these, it is helpful to glance at how some misanthropic thinkers have introduced animals into their reflections.

Rousseau, we saw, admired 'natural man', not least because of the 'pity' or compassion that such a creature felt and exercised. This 'one natural virtue' – the source of 'all the social virtues' – has atrophied since the arrival of civilisation.[6] The relevant point for us is that Rousseau praises animals for possessing this same virtue, thereby favourably comparing with 'civilised man'. Nietzsche, as we also saw, does something similar. Humankind 'represents no progress over the animal', and the 'ascent' of Christian civilisation in the West has been 'a movement of decadence'.[7] Much of Jeffers's and Baker's denunciation of humankind is inspired by their comparison of people with animals. The human race, writes the American poet, is without the 'nobility' and 'preciousness' of deer and hawk; a seal's life is 'better than ours', remarks Baker, and a falcon has the wonderful freedom that we 'fractious and smug' human beings only pretend to have.[8]

Here, then, are examples where misanthropy is suggested or confirmed by comparing the human and the animal. But it can also be inspired and reinforced by reflection on how human beings regard and treat animals. The leading contemporary advocate of the anti-natalist position discussed in Chapter 1, David Benatar, advances a 'misanthropic argument' for this position. The argument documents both our 'inhumanity' to one another and our 'brutality to "brutes"'. His chronicle of the moral crimes that people commit against animals – ranging from factory farming to experimentation – is used to support the misanthropic conclusion that 'humanity is a moral disaster'.[9] One of the reasons another author encountered earlier, Ian McHarg, regards humankind as 'a planetary disease' – a species whose elimination he 'would not feel badly' about – is people's general indifference to the fate of 'birds and bees', and their plundering and poisoning of the environments in which animals live.[10]

Unsurprisingly, an author's misanthropic attitude may be encouraged both by comparisons with animals and attention to our treatment of them. Montaigne's judgement that 'man is the most blighted' of creatures is based in part on recognising differences from animals that are unflattering to humans – the 'incomparably more lively and consistent' affection, for example, of which animals are capable. But, it is based too on his disgust at an 'inborn propensity to cruelty' towards animals, manifest for instance in the Romans' enjoyment of 'watch[ing] them tearing each other apart'.[11] In a comparable and celebrated passage from an essay on 'The Character of Man', Mark Twain wrote that 'of all the creatures that were made, man is the most detestable': he alone 'has a nasty mind' and 'possesses malice . . . the basest of all instincts, passions, vices'. He is, in addition, 'the only creature that has pain for sport, knowing it to be pain'.[12] We are worse than the animals, Twain is saying, and we treat them terribly: either is enough to condemn us. More recently, the 'natural mis-anthropy' of Mark Rowlands, referred to earlier, is fuelled by recognising that human beings are uniquely inveterate 'schemers and deceivers'. But it is then reinforced by seeing that much of their treatment of animals – in the laboratory, say – is 'a distilla-tion of human evil', a refined and intense cruelty.[13]

I said it was unsurprising that comparing humans with animals and attention to the treatment of animals sometimes combine in support of the misanthropic verdict. But actually it is more than that, for it is difficult to see how either form of reflection can fail to lead to the other. Once one starts to think about differences between humans and animals, it won't be long before one is struck, as Montaigne and Twain were, by the fact that humankind alone enjoys the infliction of pain – 'knowing it to be pain' – on other creatures. Equally, once attention is paid to the suffering to which human beings intentionally subject animals, it will soon dawn that here is a striking difference between humans and animals, one that contributes to a perception of the former as 'blighted' or 'detestable'.

It is obvious enough why the misanthrope focuses on our 'brutality to "brutes"', to the failings in our attitudes towards and treatment of animals. But some readers may wonder whether, in addition, the misanthrope needs to engage in comparisons between humans and animals. How, quite, could these add anything to the case against humankind? I want to address this and other questions about these comparisons in the remainder of the present chapter.

A LESSON FROM DAVID HUME

A good precedent for the comparisons the misanthrope wants to make is found in an essay of David Hume's, 'Of the Dignity or Meanness of Human Nature'.[14] In order to assess the extent of human dignity or meanness, Hume urges, it is necessary to compare human beings with other beings. Since there is no 'fixed unalterable standard in the nature of things', judgements of 'approbation or blame' passed on humankind can only be guided by comparison with what is non-human. In this respect, moral character is no different from, say, size. The average human being is tiny compared to a mountain, enormous compared to a microbe, and it makes no sense, without some such comparison in mind, to pronounce on the size of the average person. Likewise, the average person may be angelic relative to demons, and demonic relative to angels. Hence judgements on human 'virtue or vice', and 'merit or demerit', presuppose at least an implicit comparison with non-human beings.

In the case of their size, human beings can be compared to anything in the universe that has size. But with what might we compare humankind in the case of moral, intellectual and emotional dispositions? Hume notes that the comparison could be with angels, 'beings of the most perfect wisdom', devils and so on. But the obvious creatures with which to compare humankind are, he proposes, animals. Unlike angels and demons, animals are not only indubitably real, but 'fall under our senses'; they are visible, tangible. Angels and demons, if such there be, are not beings we can observe and inspect, and it is all too easy, therefore, to invest them with whatever properties we like, which makes any comparison between them and ourselves skewed from the outset. They are not, so to speak, genuine control groups. That we can imagine 'beings of the most perfect wisdom', Hume writes, is a poor reason for judging that humankind is very stupid. Likewise, that I can imagine demons who greatly surpass us in their malevolence is a bad reason to conclude that we are, after all, not so bad as we feared. Solid flesh-and-blood animals, 'falling under our senses' as they do, resist wilful attribution to them of properties. Because of this, comparisons with animals in order to ascertain the dignity or meanness of humankind can be objectively made.

When Hume writes that the kind of comparison truly 'worth our attention' enables us to judge 'the motives or actuating principles of human nature', he is making a further, and important, point. It is not simply that, in the absence of comparison with animals, there is no measure for arriving at verdicts on humankind. Comparing similarities and differences between the human and the animal also enables us to identify, or at any rate render salient, aspects of human existence that would otherwise be unnoticed or only dimly discerned, their importance unrecognised. Comparison, then, is not a matter simply of checking the features of one kind of creature against those of another, for it is only through comparison that it is possible to draw up lists of all the relevant features in the first place. For example, prior to reflection on how animal lives differ from our own, it is hardly obvious what a distinctive, central role in human existence the concepts of past and future have. Nor, as Rousseau saw, would it be obvious, in the absence of a contrast with animals, just how important to men and women is the practice of comparing themselves with one another in an attempt to boost or protect their self-esteem. (I'll return to these and other distinctive aspects of human being in Chapter 3.)

David Hume, certainly, was no misanthrope. He is at least as critical, in his essay, of those who 'discover nothing, except vanity, in which man surpasses the other animals' as of those who 'exalt our species to the skies'. Indeed, he thinks the comparison with animals is, overall, distinctly 'favourable to mankind'. Misanthropes will reject this conclusion, preferring the spirit, at least, of the French revolutionary, Mme Roland's remark, 'The more I see of man, the more I admire dogs'.[15] They will certainly agree with those, like Konrad Lorenz, for whom comparing humans and animals soon dents a perception of humankind as 'standing apart as a higher being'.[16] What misanthropes learn from Hume, however, is the significance and indispensability for their appraisal of humankind, of exploring its likeness and unlikeness to other kinds of creature.

HUMAN ANIMALS?

There's a worry that some people have with speaking of a comparison between humans and animals. Mary Midgley's celebrated book, Beast and Man, begins with the proclamation that 'We are not just rather like animals; we are animals'.[17] To compare humans with animals, therefore, rests on a category mistake: it's as if one were to compare Germans with Europeans. If a philosopher distinguishes between people and animals, another author tells us, 'it is best to skip that part of his thesis'.[18]

It is true, of course, that human beings are animals in the sense of being living creatures that ingest and metabolise matter, are sentient and move themselves around. But it's equally and self-evidently true that people are not animals if the term is defined, as in the OED, as 'a brute or beast, as distinguished from man'. This second sense is, moreover, very familiar and indeed the predominant one in ordinary discourse. If I tell you that there are two animals next door, referring to a married couple, what I say is a joke or an insult, not a plain statement of fact.

So, is it simply a trivial, verbal issue whether human beings are counted as animals? Those who insist on so counting them are typically concerned to reduce the gap that, as they see it, people in the past perceived between humans and animals. They are keen to tell us, for example, that people are not set apart from animals by possessing an immortal soul, or by having been made in the image of God. That may be right, as is the claim that human beings share many needs and feelings with animals. But it is hard to see that insisting, complete with italics, that we *are* animals does anything by itself to assimilate human life to that of (non-human) animals, and to counter what is sometimes labelled 'human exceptionalism'.[19]

We saw, when discussing the idea of human nature in Chapter 1, that people do not belong to just one, biological kind: they are a kind of animal, but they are also persons, members therefore of what is not a biological category at all. When one author begins his book with the words 'Human beings are animals . . .', he quickly completes the sentence with the words ' . . . with a distinctive range of abilities', and then proceeds to identify capacities that he takes to be distinctively human, including linguistic and cognitive ones.[20] So, yes, humans are animals but maybe very, very special ones, fundamentally different from other animals in most important respects. Conversely, reluctance to call human beings 'animals' – due, say, to the pejorative figurative senses that may cling to the word – is perfectly compatible with holding that, in nearly all significant respects, we are strikingly similar to animals, and that our distinctive abilities are not of great moment.

The question whether we are animals or not is, then, a rather tedious one. Whichever answer is given does nothing to settle the interesting question of how human beings resemble and differ from (non-human) animals. Since it would also be tedious to keep inserting '(non-human)' before 'animals' when it is (non-human) animals that I am discussing, in the rest of the book I shall generally leave it out. Readers whose sensitivities are offended by this policy are free to visualise '(non-human)' each time they see the word 'animal(s)'.

WHICH ANIMALS?

Zoologists and other animal experts sometimes complain that philosophers fail, when talking about animals, properly to distinguish among different species. There are, after all, around nine million animal species, according to one recent count. There are far fewer species of mammal, but more than enough – around 5,500 – to make plenty of generalisations about mammals suspect.

The misanthrope will be asked, then, which animals are intended when we are invited to reflect on their relationships with humankind. The short answer to the question of which animals the misanthrope compares human beings with might be this: dogs – and whatever animals are like dogs in ways relevant to the misanthrope's comparison. Little of interest by way of an appraisal of human failings is likely to emerge from comparing people with creatures – worms, say, or butterflies – whose lives are so unlike our own that the comparison could as well be with plants. That butterflies are not cruel, vain, dishonest or wilfully ignorant doesn't count in favour of their superiority over us any more than the absence of these failings in tulips could count in favour of theirs. For comparisons to be instructive, they need to be with animals whose lives are sufficiently rich and complex for it to make sense to speculate on their virtues and failings. Dogs, wolves and elephants nicely fit the bill: they are social creatures, equipped with a range of emotions, forms of understanding and powers of communication. It is because they are creatures of this type that, in various cultures, their lives have been closely integrated with those of human beings.

There is no need for the misanthrope to be at all precise, in advance, as to the animals with which comparisons will be made, since it will depend upon context and angle of interest – on the particular human failings being investigated – which are the most suitable to consider. In respectively assessing human cruelty and vanity, for example, it may be different animals with which comparison is most usefully made.

It might be asked why the misanthrope identifies dogs as paradigmatic of the kinds of animal with which to compare ourselves, and not the animals with whom we share a common ancestor and over 99% of our genetic make-up – chimpanzees and other apes. Rousseau thought that orangutans shared what he proposed as the defining feature of human beings – a capacity to try to improve or 'perfect' themselves – and should therefore be classed together with 'natural men'.[21] He may have been wrong about both orangutans and the defining feature of human beings, but there are two morals to be drawn from Rousseau's discussion.

First, comparisons with animals for the purpose of appraising humankind should not be dictated by biological, genetic considerations. The misanthrope's interest, rather, is in the conduct of life. The obvious physical similarities between humans and chimpanzees are of less interest to the misanthrope than, say, similarities in family relationships – and these may be more significant in the case of wolves or elephants than of chimpanzees. Second, the reason Rousseau wants to lump orangutans together, rather than compare them, with 'natural men' is because there is insufficient contrast between them for comparison to be instructive. And this suggests that the many obvious similarities between apes and ourselves means that the differences have less salience than the misanthrope wants from comparisons designed to bring human failings into relief. In identifying these failings, therefore, the misanthrope does well, for much of the time, to focus on creatures whose differences from ourselves are, if not greater, then at least more visible, than in the case of fellow primates.

The question 'Which animals?' arises, too, in connection with the misanthrope's reflections on our treatment of animals. The short answer to the question is 'All animals that are or might be treated wrongly by human beings'. A different answer is given by people inspired by Jeremy Bentham's famous remark that the only relevant issue when it comes to treatment of animals is 'Can they suffer?'.[22] For them, the only animals to consider, therefore, are those capable of suffering at our hands. But this answer mistakenly suggests that the only way animals can be treated badly is by being caused to suffer. Humiliating an elephant, mocking a cat, betraying a dog's trust, or using a dead hedgehog as a football may cause no suffering, but they are wrong ways to treat animals. Even creatures that may be incapable of suffering can be treated wrongly, as when someone chops a worm into pieces or takes the wings off a fly just for the fun of it. Someone might reply that such actions are no worse than the pointless destruction of flowers or bushes. Possibly not, but that's bad enough.

Since it is possible to imagine wrongful treatment of any animal at all, however small or low in the zoological hierarchy, maybe the answer to the question as to which animals the misanthrope should be considering is, simply, 'All animals'. There is, of course, a much smaller class of animals, capable of great suffering and other forms of feeling and awareness, that are victims of the worst treatments that humankind metes out. So, in later chapters, it will, unsurprisingly, be dogs, chickens, bears or mice rather than ants, worms or midges that occupy our attention. It was animals in this smaller class, we saw, who are also the ones that the misanthrope has in mind when comparing human and animal lives. It's to this comparison that we now turn.

NOTES

1 Thomas Macaulay, *History of England*, Vol. 1, Chapter lii. www.endnotes.com/topics/history-england/quotes. Accessed 15/05/2017.

2 Steven Pinker, *The Better Angels of Our Nature*, London: Penguin, 2011, p. 556.

3 Robinson Jeffers, *Selected Poems*, Manchester: Carcanet, 1987, p. 35.

4 J. A. Baker, *The Peregrine*, New York: New York Review of Books, 2005, p. 144.

5 Mary Midgley, *Animals and Why They Matter*, London: Penguin, 1983, p. 31.

6 Jean-Jacques Rousseau, *Discourse on the Origin of Inequality*, Oxford: Oxford University Press, 1994, p. 45.

7 Nietzsche, *The Will to Power*, New York: Vintage, 1968, § 90.

8 Jeffers, *Selected Poems*, pp. 90, 92; Baker, *The Peregrine*, pp. 28, 128.

9 David Benatar and David Wasserman, *Debating Procreation: Is It Wrong to Procreate?* Oxford: Oxford University Press, 2015, p. 111.

10 Ian McHarg, *Man: The Planetary Disease*, B.Y. Morrison Memorial Lecture, Washington, DC: Agriculture Research Service, pp. 1, 3.

11 Michel de Montaigne, *The Complete Essays*, London: Penguin, 1991, pp. 485, 505, 525.

12 Mark Twain, *What Is Man? And Other Philosophical Writings*, Berkeley, CA: University of California Press, 1973, p. 60.

13 Mark Rowlands, *The Philosopher and the Wolf*, London: Granta, 2008, pp. 63, 92, 104.

14 David Hume, 'Of the Dignity or Meanness of Human Nature', in his *Essays: Moral Political and Literary*, Oxford: Oxford University Press, 1963, pp. 81–8.

15 For this and similar quotes from, among many others, Mme de Stael and Lamartine, see www.dogquotations.com.

16 Konrad Lorenz, *On Aggression*, London: Routledge, 2002, p. 219.

17 Mary Midgley, *Beast and Man: The Roots of Human Nature*, London: Methuen, 1980, p. xiii.

18 Vicki Hearne, *Animal Happiness*, New York: Skyhorse (Kindle ed.), 2007, Introduction.

19 Aaron Gross, 'Introduction and Overview: Animal Others and Animal Studies', in A. Gross and A. Vallely (eds.), *Animals and the Human Imagination: A Companion to Animal Studies*, New York: Columbia University Press, p. 1.

20 P. M. S. Hacker, *Human Nature: The Categorial Framework*, Oxford: Wiley-Blackwell, 2010, p. 1.

21 Rousseau, *Discourse on the Origin of Inequality*, p. 105.

22 Jeremy Bentham, *Introduction to the Principles of Moral and Legislation*, Oxford: Oxford University Press, 1907, Chapter 17, n. 122.

3

HUMAN AND ANIMAL LIVES

The misanthrope wants to compare human virtues and failings with those that animals may possess. But comparison must begin further back, with differences and affinities between human and animal lives that are presupposed by any broadly moral comparison. There are aspects peculiar to human life without which certain failings would be impossible – failings, therefore, that it would make no sense to attribute to animals. Conversely, there are important affinities between human and animal lives that justify comparisons of the kind the misanthrope intends. What follows in this chapter is not a comprehensive survey of the kinship or lack of it between humans and animals. I am concerned to identify only those differences and affinities relevant to the misanthrope's programme.

DIFFERENCES

From possession of an immortal soul to having a sense of humour, from being language users to a liability to fall in love . . .

any number of features have been cited as setting human beings apart from all animals. Some of them are genuine differences, some are not. In this section, I identify some genuine and fundamental differences between our existence and that of animals – fundamental, since many further differences depend upon them.

Let me begin with the uniquely human relationship to time. Nietzsche wrote that 'animals are contained in the present', Schopenhauer that animals are the 'present incarnate'.[1] Their point is not that a dog cannot remember where he hid the bone, or anticipate that he is about to be taken for a walk. Rather, the point is one about the connection between time and self-consciousness. Self-consciousness is often taken to be a defining feature of human beings, but this is clearly false in some perfectly ordinary senses of the expression. The pigeon knows that it's *she* whom the hawk is about to attack; the dog recognises *himself* in the mirror; the cat becomes uncomfortably aware that I'm staring at *her*, not her brother. Self-consciousness is not a single notion, and when understood as, for example, self-recognition or self-attention, there is no reason to confine it to human beings. The form of self-consciousness that is confined to us could be called 'consciousness of self' – a phrase too portentous to apply to the pigeon's fear of the impending attack, or the dog's recognising himself in the mirror.[2]

Self-consciousness in the shape of consciousness of self requires a sense of time that extends indefinitely into the past and future. To be conscious of myself, of being the person I am, I must be able to recognise myself as someone who, say, went to a certain university so many years ago, and as someone – the same someone – who in the future will need another knee operation. A dog, by contrast, can remember burying the bone an hour ago and look forward to an imminent walk, but there is nothing the dog can do to suggest that he recognises that it was he who got hit by a car some years ago, and that it is he who will one day become old and grey.

It is because dogs and other animals are lacking in temporally extended self-consciousness that they cannot be described as nostalgic or remorseful, optimistic or plagued with angst about the future. That they can't be so described is, in turn, a good reason for holding that they lack this form of self-consciousness. To be sure, there can be honest disagreements as to which feelings and experiences animals are precluded from through 'just being, here and now', as the garden writer Monty Don puts it. I'm not sure, for example, that Don is right to think that his dog, Nigel's lack of a sense of a temporally extended self means that he cannot feel guilt.[3] It is clear, however, that neither Nigel nor any other animal can sensibly be accused of such failings as cloying sentimentality about the past and irresponsible nonchalance about the future. These failings, at least, are a human prerogative.

A second important feature unique to human beings – one that presupposes the sense of time just discussed – is what Rousseau called *amour-propre*. Sometimes translated as 'vanity', it is this, he thinks, that decisively distinguishes 'civilised man' from 'natural man', orangutans and all other animals. *Amour-propre* is contrasted with *amour de soi-même* (love of one's self), the 'natural sentiment that prompts every animal' to preserve and defend itself. Vanity, on the other hand, is a product of civilisation, the 'artificial sentiment that prompts each individual to set greater store by himself than by anyone else'.[4] It is egoistic in a way that the instinct of self-preservation, *amour de soi-même*, is not.

A creature cannot be guilty of *amour-propre* if it lacks a temporally extended sense of self. I cannot set more store by myself than by any other person unless I have beliefs about my past and future. I cannot, for instance, hold myself in high esteem if I believe that I have always been and always will be one of life's failures. Animals, unable to identify themselves with the beings they once were and one day will be, cannot compare themselves on a scale of self-esteem.

For Rousseau, *amour-propre* is not an isolated evil of civilised life, but a precondition for most of our failings and vices. It 'triggers all the evil men do', he writes.[5] People who act out of envy or resentment, for example, are typically driven by a sense that the world does not set the same store by them as they deserve. Envy and resentment, at least of this kind, cannot therefore be motives for the behaviour of animals.

A concern with esteem is an ingredient in a third and wider aspect of human being that distinguishes it from that of animals. The ever-helpful Rousseau gives a clue to this aspect. Human beings are distinguished from animals – except those 'honorary' human beings, orangutans ('wise old men of the forest') – by a 'capacity as free agent(s) . . . for perfectibility' or 'self-improvement'.[6] Rousseau's choice of terms is not ideal, given his conviction that nearly all attempts by civilised man to exercise this capacity are a disaster. The point he is getting at, however, is a valid one that was better expressed by Martin Heidegger in his account of *Dasein* ('being there'). This is his name for the kind of being that human beings, but not animals, have. One of the defining features of this kind of being is that it is an 'issue' for each creature – each person, in effect – who has it.[7]

Where the next meal is coming from, or how to fend off a predator, may be an issue, a matter of concern, for a mouse or sparrow. But it is only human beings, with their extended awareness of time, who can be concerned and anxious about the kind of beings they are. The kind of person you are matters to you. The direction of your life, the possibilities open to you to change this direction, the value of what you have achieved, how to put your life in better order – these are issues of concern for you in a way they could not be for your pet cat.

Like the other distinguishing aspects of human existence, that our lives are an 'issue' for us, is a precondition for a range of failings and virtues. Only a creature able to reflect on the nature and direction of its life can be self-pitying, self-deceptive and irresponsible – or, instead, display self-honesty and resoluteness. In Heidegger's terminology, only a human life can be authentic or inauthentic, according to whether a person grasps or fails to grasp – reflects or fails to reflect upon – the issue that this life confronts the person with.

Part of reflection on one's life is, broadly understood, moral reflection. And here is the final distinctive aspect of human life I want to identify. Only human beings have a reflective moral sense, for only they have the conceptual repertoire that this requires. This is not to say that only human beings can act viciously or virtuously. Whether or not animals can do so is an important question that I address in a later chapter. Suppose they can. Suppose, say, that they can be cruel and compassionate. It won't follow that they therefore exercise the concepts of cruelty and compassion, or that they have a reflective moral sense. Indeed, it seems clear that they do not, for these concepts and this sense are embedded in forms of social life led by creatures capable of self-conscious awareness of their intentions, motives and purposes. To understand cruelty, for example, is to understand that it involves the intentional infliction of unnecessary pain for a reason – pleasure, say, or spite – other than the anticipated good of the victim.

Once more, this aspect of human existence is presupposed by many distinctively human failings. Only creatures who know what rights and duties are can violate rights and shirk their duties. Reneging on promises, betrayal of trust, hypocrisy, ignoring the voice of conscience . . . the list goes on of behaviour that can be engaged in only by creatures with a conceptual repertoire that allows for moral reflection and deliberation.

Three comments are worth making on the distinctive capacities of human beings that I have identified. First, while these capacities are universal, the degree to which and the ways in which they are exercised may vary considerably from one society or culture to another. We are rightly warned not to make unqualified references to the form of human life.[8] There were and still are, for example, traditional tribal societies in which it is not expected of people that they engage in individual moral reflection or regard the future as theirs to shape. But this is not to say that members of such societies lack the capacities to do so.

Second, the aspects of human existence I've discussed are more fundamental than some of the candidates, such as laughter and art, that are sometimes proposed for distinguishing human from animal lives. They are fundamental because, as we have seen, so many further differences between the human and the animal – including laughter and art – presuppose them. This makes popular slogans like 'We are just animals' and 'Humans are only one animal species among many' ring hollow. Earlier, I suggested that the question whether we are animals or not is a tedious one, the interesting question being instead about the similarities and differences between humans and (non-human) animals. The popular slogans are guilty, surely, of masking what are real and profound differences.

Third, I don't pretend that my list of fundamental differences is exhaustive. I have identified only those that will be most relevant to the misanthrope's discussion of our relations with animals. When the Daoist sage, Zhuangzi, remarked that human beings, unlike fish confined to their pond, 'wander' through the whole world and 'take heaven and earth as their palace', he meant that the range of human interest and enquiry is unlimited. It is not circumscribed by the particular environments in which people find themselves.[9] If this is right then here, surely, is a large difference between the human and the animal, but it is not one that will figure – not prominently, at least – in the misanthrope's reflections.

AFFINITIES

Important as it is to identify aspects distinctive of humankind, it is equally so to consider ones that are shared with many animals.

Without recognition of these affinities, misanthropes cannot proceed with either their comparison of the human and the animal or their exposure of the wrongs inflicted on animals.

A good strategy for identifying affinities is through rejecting a number of differences that have been wrongly alleged to distinguish human beings from all animals. I'll be brief with these allegations since not only are they uncompelling, but the more interesting task (for later in the chapter) is to diagnose why they have been made in the first place.[10] Certainly, one can be brief with the extreme claim that animals differ from us in lacking any kind of consciousness, including awareness of pleasure and pain. This is a claim made by some followers of Descartes in the seventeenth century (though not by Descartes himself),[11] and adopted as a supposedly useful working hypothesis by twentieth-century behaviourist psychologists. Scepticism about the existence of animal consciousness is still occasionally heard from scientists, including one who, when looking at an elephant in an African game reserve, remarked 'I have no way of knowing whether that elephant is any more conscious than this bush'.[12] More often, it is heard from anglers and hunters keen to convince people, and perhaps themselves, that their hobby causes no suffering to the creatures they hook, trap or shoot.

That animals are, or might be, completely lacking in awareness is something that hardly anyone can seriously believe. The claim is typically disingenuous, self-serving 'bullshit' that people making it don't even attempt to substantiate – either that or a symptom of lunacy. For we see animals suffering pain, enjoying their food or being frightened by sudden noises with the same clarity and certainty that we observe this in our friends and children. Those who feel the need to buttress what is searingly obvious to us in our ordinary dealings with animals can turn to the many scientific studies that show how animals' brains release the same chemicals, such as dopamine and serotonin, that ours do when we experience pleasures and pains.[13]

For some people, this is where the concession to animal mind-edness should end. Yes, they say, animals are sensate, but probably no more than that. Such deniers or sceptics cannot accept, for example, that animals are capable of emotions and moods, accusing those who describe a dog as 'bored', say, of 'anthropomorphism'.[14] But it is only a ritual, professional scepticism that could prevent someone from recognising boredom, anger, depression, gratitude and happiness in the eyes, faces, gestures and behaviour of dogs, monkeys and other animals. It might take more expert observation to recognise the emotions and moods of, say, ravens, but those who work on corvids have no doubt as to the birds' capacity for anger, affection and much else.

Even an expert who has 'no doubt' that a raven is a 'feeling being' may express doubt, however, as to whether it is also 'a thinking being'.[15] Maybe Descartes was right to deny that any animal is 'a thinking thing'. So, perhaps the concessions to animal consciousness should stop with the attribution only of affective experience – feelings, moods, emotions. But if a thinking being is a creature that displays intelligence and exercises concepts in recognising things *as* trees, prey or whatever, then ravens and countless other creatures are thinking beings. It is no more plausible to doubt that some animals understand and reason than to doubt that they have feelings and emotions. Indeed, many moods and emotions that we are happy to attribute to animals presuppose their intelligence and understanding. A dog can't be disappointed at not finding his bone unless he knows what a bone is and what it is to search for one. An elephant can't demonstrate compassion for another, wounded elephant unless it recognises that it is a wounded elephant, a fellow creature in need of help, and understands how to comfort it.

It is only by operating with inflated, over-intellectualised conceptions of thought, understanding and intelligence that it is possible to doubt that animals are capable of these. One such inflated conception requires a creature deemed capable of understanding to be the user of a language. My dog, it gets argued, cannot genuinely *believe* that his bone is under the tree, since to believe something is to hold a statement to be true.[16] Dogs, however, don't even recognise statements, let alone hold them to be true or false. But on no familiar conception of belief and understanding is it seriously in question that dogs understand things and have beliefs. Rather than question if my dog believes I'm about to feed it one should challenge the peculiar proposal that belief is a matter of taking statements as true.

Challenged, too, should be the equally strange, but familiar view that, since animals cannot tell us what they think, then there is no reason to suppose they do think. What makes the view strange is this: someone who doubts that the behaviour of a creature, human or animal, can show what it believes should surely extend this doubt to the particular form of behaviour we call speaking. In fact, it is probably easier to programme an unthinking robot to emit what sound like linguistic utterances than to emulate the gestures, facial expressions and bodily movements that we ordinarily and rightly take as manifestations of intelligence and thought.

Is it anyway true that, as many allege, animals have no language? It is not relevant to this question to argue about the findings of experiments that test the ability of gorillas and chimpanzees to manipulate and combine symbols. For the question is not what a few animals might be able to do in artificial circumstances, but what many animals typically and effortlessly do in their natural settings. They don't, of course, deploy complex systems of signs that are governed by syntactic and semantic rules – languages, that is, in the sense in which English and Bengali are languages. But we happily refer, and without a sense of speaking figuratively, to the language of whales, birds and other creatures. Animals use language in the sense of intentionally communicating with one another about their world and themselves.

The animal trainer and philosopher Vicki Hearne writes of the 'rich and subtle conversations' she has with her horse, of exchanging signs – primarily through touch, a language 'of the skin' – and of their shared 'participation' in a 'loop of intention and openness'. Language, she holds, is essentially this kind of participation. Languages, like English and Bengali, are only particular, highly structured forms through which to conduct this participation. Far from language being a uniquely human faculty, she concludes, dogs or horses may have a greater mastery of language – measured by ease of participation, of reciprocity and openness – than most of us have, and certainly greater than that of the gorilla struggling to combine plastic symbols into structured sequences.[17]

These remarks bear directly on another alleged difference between people and animals. It's been argued that no animal is capable of 'I-contact', of seeing human beings as 'intentional systems' and hence of attributing beliefs or desires to them.[18] I'm not sure what it is to see another person as an intentional system, but if the claim is that animals can never recognise what a person thinks or wants, then it is wrong. Animals might not be good at 'mind-reading' (are we?), but they can be very good at 'body-reading' – of recognising, like Vicki Hearne's horse, what someone intends or wants in their movement, gesture and touch.[19] One philosopher perceptively compares the 'unspoken dialogue of expression and gesture' that enables an animal and a person to 'make sense' of one another to a dance, in which the partners communicate an intention by a slight twist of the body or pressure of the hand.[20] Here is a more appropriate model for 'I-contact' – for mutual understanding or intersubjectivity – than that of hypothesising what is happening inside an intentional system.

Two brief concluding remarks on these bogus differences between the human and the animals. First, I have said nothing about a further alleged difference – the absence, in animals, of a capacity to act morally. Since the truth or otherwise of this allegation is obviously central to the misanthrope's broadly moral comparison of humankind with animals, discussion of it is postponed until Chapter 5, when this comparison is underway. Second, while the best writers on our engagement with animals are in no doubt as to the absurdity of the claim – by a follower of Descartes – that animals 'eat without pleasure, cry without pain, grow without knowing it, desire nothing, fear nothing, know nothing',[21] they also emphasise the opacity, the mystery even, of animal lives. It is one thing to know that my dog is joyfully happy today, quite another to imagine just how the world figures for him when he is so happy. This is a point relevant to ways in which we should strive to be with, to engage with, animals – a topic for Chapter 9.

SCEPTICISM, THEORY AND LIFE

More interesting than refutation of wrong-headed claims about differences between the human and the animal, I suggested, is diagnosis of the reasons that inspire such claims. (The two are related, of course, for to discredit these reasons is to further undermine confidence in the claims.) Here are some of them.

Historically, a number of religious and associated metaphysical doctrines have contributed to an intellectual climate in which differences between animals and humans are invented or exaggerated. One thinks, for example, of the Platonic, Christian and Cartesian conviction that the seat of thought and reason is an immaterial soul, separable from the body in which it is lodged and peculiar to human beings. Or the Islamic and Christian doctrine that human beings alone are created in the image of God. Or the Buddhist doctrine that bad people are reborn as animals that – until being reborn as people once more – cannot attain enlightenment.

Of greater contemporary interest is what Mary Midgley labelled a 'ritual scepticism' towards animals adopted by scientists in the name of objectivity.[22] The force of the term 'ritual' is to question whether the professed scepticism is genuine and considered. One wonders, for example, how a scientist can maintain scepticism towards animal intelligence while at the same time approving a primatologist's remark that 'only by looking at the gorillas as living, feeling beings was I able to enter into the life of the group with comprehension, instead of remaining an ignorant spectator'.[23] The quoted remark is an implicit criticism, moreover, of the ritual sceptic's tendency to suppose that it is essentially through just observing animals – preferably in the controlled context of a laboratory or zoo – that we gain knowledge about them, rather than through engaging with them, participating in their lives. Objectivity is not a virtue when it excludes the very ways of relating to animals most apt to produce understanding of them. Imagine how a man's wife and children would react to his refusal to accept, despite his sharing the home with them, that they were intelligent, emotional beings until experimental evidence confirmed this.

Contributing to ritual scepticism is a misleading image of thought and feeling as inner, private processes that need to be inferred from the overt behaviour of creatures. The ritual sceptic's tactic, typically, is to regard judgements about feelings and thoughts as 'hypotheses' that need to be verified, and then to announce that, of course, they cannot be, since we have no access to the private sphere in which they occur. But in ordinary circumstances, no such hypotheses or need for confirmation are involved. Only where there is some specific ground for doubt is it legitimate to speak of hypothesis and verification. It may be hard to tell, on some occasion, if the man (or dog) is feigning aggression or if it's for real. In such cases, one waits and watches, hoping that the man (or dog) does something to show just what his mood or intention is. Where there is no such ground for doubt, I simply see that, for example, the child is happy with the toy it's been given, that the dog is working out how to retrieve its bone or that the giraffe wants to reach the top branch of the tree. Except on a peculiarly impoverished conception of what we can see in the faces, movements and gestures of humans and animals alike, it is clear that we directly experience creatures as intelligent, feeling beings. With animals as with humans, to amend a remark of Wittgenstein's, the body is the best picture of the soul.[24]

The quaint image of us constantly trying to verify hypotheses about inner, private states exemplifies a wider tendency that exaggerates differences between humans and animals. This is the tendency to over-intellectualise and treat our understanding of animals as theoretical in character. Consider, here, the use by ritual sceptics of theoretically inflated concepts of belief, language, emotion and much else that bear little resemblance to those we employ in our ordinary experience of animals. We've already met with several of these: the idea of belief as an attitude towards a statement, of language as a rule-governed system, or of reciprocal understanding as matter of attributing mental states to 'intentional systems', for example. Other excessively theoretical concepts that encourage exaggeration of differences between human and animal psychologies include that of meaning something as requiring a complex set of intentions, and the notion that to know something a creature must know that it knows.

In everyday discourse, whether about animals or human beings, 'belief', 'knowledge', 'meaning', 'language', 'emotion' and the rest are not theoretical terms. They owe their sense to the ways in which they are unreflectingly and effortlessly employed in what Wittgenstein called 'the stream of life'.[25] Like most ordinary terms, they are used to respond to and guide our practical engagement with the world in which we move and act. When so used, they are applied unhesitatingly to animals, many of which are important members of the world with which farmers, dog owners, gardeners or bird-watchers engage. Only in special circumstances will these people pause before talking of a cow's concern for her calf, a dog's meaning to attract attention, a hedgehog's fear of being attacked or a bird's affection for its mate.

What this frictionless use of a rich psychological vocabulary in describing animals shows is that we recognise that they, like ourselves, have lives and worlds of their own. A cat is not simply alive, but leads a life, replete with concerns and purposes. A fox is not simply in an environment, like a bush, but *has* an environment, a sphere or world of significance in which things figure for the fox as meaningful – as things to avoid, eat, play with, nurture and much else. Cat and fox don't just inhabit a certain space. As the great Japanese haiku poet, Issa, often notes, creatures – even butterflies and fleas – do not simply live, they have to 'make a living' in their world.[26] Or, as the pioneering biologist and animal ethologist, Jakob von Uexküll, puts it, they participate in Umwelten, contexts or little worlds in which the things they encounter and have dealings with are 'carriers of meaning'.[27] It is in and through having lives and worlds that animals display their most fundamental affinity with human beings.

None of this erases the important differences between human and animal lives identified earlier in this chapter. But nor should these differences – let alone the bogus ones rejected over the last few pages – impede recognition of the fundamental affinity from which all further affinities flow. Emotional response, mood, understanding of things, communication of intentions, empathy, 'body-reading' . . . these are ways in which animals, like human beings, adjust and negotiate their dealings with their worlds and the fellow creatures who inhabit them. In a fine passage at the end of his book on the minds of animals, the ecologist Carl Safina writes that we and animals share

> a common quest: to live, to raise our young, to find space enough for our lives, to survive the confronting dangers, to do

> what it takes . . . to live out the mystery and opportunity of find-
> ing ourselves somehow in existence.[28]

I have only to look out of my study window at the sparrows, tits and finches feeding their young at the bird-table in our garden to recognise the truth in those words.

NOTES

1 Quoted in Joshua Foa Dienstag, *Philosophy, Ethic, Spirit*, Princeton, NJ: Princeton University Press, 2006, p. 20. Dienstag argues that, for philosophical pessimists, it is human 'consciousness of time' that is responsible for most of our ills.

2 On animal self-consciousness, see Frans de Waal, *Are We Smart Enough to Know How Smart Animals Are?* London: Granta, 2016.

3 Monty Don, *Nigel: My Family and Other Dogs*, London: Two Roads, 2016, p. 70.

4 Jean-Jacques Rousseau, *Discourse on the Origin of Inequality*, Oxford: Oxford University Press, 1994, p. 115.

5 Ibid., p. 117.

6 Ibid., p. 105.

7 Martin Heidegger, *Being and Time*, Oxford: Blackwell, 1980, pp. 67–8.

8 See Mikel Burley, 'Eating Human Beings: Varieties of Cannibalism and the Heterogeneity of Human Life', *Philosophy*, 91, 2016, pp. 483–501.

9 See Franklin Perkins, 'Of Fish and Men: Species Difference and the Strangeness of Being Human in *Zhuangzi*', *Harvard Review of Philosophy*, XVI, 2010, pp. 118–36.

10 Many books provide detailed and compelling refutations of the alleged differences, including Marc Bekoff, *The Emotional Lives of Animals*, New York: New World Library, 2009; Lynne Sharpe, *Creatures Like Us: A Relational Approach to the Moral Status of Animals*, Exeter: Imprint Academia, 2005; Frans de Waal, *Are We Smart Enough to Know How Smart*

Animals Are? and Carl Safina, *Beyond Words: What Animals Think*, London: Souvenir, 2015.

11 See John Cottingham, '"A Brute to Beasts"? Descartes' Treatment of Animals', *Philosophy*, 53, 1978, pp. 551–60.

12 Quoted in Safina, *Beyond Words*, p. 19.

13 See, in addition to the works listed in n. 10 above, Jonathan Balcombe, *Pleasurable Kingdom: Animals and the Nature of Feeling Good*, London: Palgrave Macmillan, 2007.

14 See Jeffrey Masson, *Dogs Never Lie about Love*, London: Vintage, 1997, p. 92.

15 Bernd Heinrich, *Mind of the Raven*, New York: HarperCollins, 2006, p. 45.

16 See Donald Davidson, 'Thought and Talk', in his *Inquiries into Truth and Interpretation*, Oxford: Oxford University Press, 2001, pp. 155–70.

17 Vicki Hearne, *Adam's Task: Calling Animals by Name*, New York: Skyhorse, 2007, pp. 42, 85, 112.

18 Roger Scruton, *On Human Nature*, Princeton, NJ: Princeton University Press, 2017, p. 36.

19 On body-reading, see de Waal, *Are We Smart Enough to Know How Smart Animals Are?* p. 132.

20 Simon P. James, *The Presence of Nature*, Basingstoke: Palgrave Macmillan, 2009, p. 42. Chapter 2 of this book is an excellent dissection of the bogus differences between animals and people I have been discussing.

21 Nicolas Malebranche, quoted in James, *The Presence of Nature*, p. 47.

22 Mary Midgley, *Animals and Why They Matter*, London: Penguin, 1983, p. 137.

23 Heinrich, *Mind of the Raven*, p. 335. The primatologist quoted is George Schaller.

24 Ludwig Wittgenstein, *Philosophical Investigations*, London: Palgrave Macmillan, 1969, p. 178e.

25 Ludwig Wittgenstein, *Zettel*, Oxford: Blackwell, 1975, § 173. For criticism of the over-theoretical accounts of beliefs, desires and so

on of which psychologists are fond, see Matthew Ratcliffe, *Rethinking Commonsense Psychology: A Critique of Folk Psychology, Theory of Mind and Simulation*, New York: Palgrave Macmillan, 2007.

26 In David G. Lanoue, *Issa and the Meaning of Animals: A Buddhist Poet's Perspective*, New Orleans: HaikuGuy.com, 2014, e.g. pp. 107, 110.

27 Jakob von Uexküll, *A Foray into the Worlds of Animals and Human: With a Theory of Meaning*, Minneapolis: University of Minnesota Press, 2010.

28 Safina, *Beyond Words*, p. 411.

4

HUMAN FAILINGS

The identification of differences and affinities between human and animal life was a necessary prelude to the broadly moral comparison that is the misanthrope's aim. This comparison will confirm the spirit of Mme Roland's remark that the more she sees of men, the more she admires dogs – or, as she might have said, the more she sees of dogs, the less she admires humankind. The misanthrope wants to show that human life is saturated with failings in a way that animal life is not. In the present chapter, the misanthrope draws up a list of these failings, and argues that they are ubiquitous, entrenched and distinctively human. But first some brief reminders of earlier points.

REMINDERS

First, a reminder of the irksome matter, raised in Chapter 1, of terminology. I have already referred to the misanthrope's *broadly* moral comparison of the human and the animal. The adverb registers that 'moral', left unqualified, is too narrow a term, especially as used in contemporary moral philosophy, for the parameters of the misanthrope's comparison. Some of the failings identified would be better described as spiritual, aesthetic, emotional or intellectual, but it would be tedious to keep repeating these terms, so I'll sometimes abbreviate them to broadly moral failings.

'Failings', I also noted, is a bland term, but at least it has the required breadth. 'Vice' is too closely tied to specifically moral wrong to have the necessary generality. That said, many failings the misanthrope identifies are reasonably described as moral vices so that, despite its somewhat archaic tone, I'll use the term when appropriate. The word 'virtue' is less problematic, since it has escaped from its confinement to the sphere of morality. We now comfortably speak of such virtues as cleanliness and clear-sightedness. 'Virtue', in effect, is not the opposite of 'vice', but of the more general term 'failing', and that is how I shall use it. The archaic tone of the vocabulary of virtue is not, incidentally, entirely unwelcome, for it was a notion central to the ancient Greek, Indian and Chinese reflections on the good life on which the misanthrope frequently draws. Virtues were dispositions that contributed to or even constituted the good life. Vices, or more generally failings, were those that obstructed it.

Despite differences in religious and metaphysical doctrine, there was considerable agreement among the ancients on what traits were virtuous or vicious. Confucians, Stoics and Buddhists could all agree on the virtues of courage and equanimity, and on the vices of greed and hubris. And, to recall what I said earlier, I take it that all of us can broadly agree on this and much else. Few people would deny that on any viable conception of the good life – of a life that is realised and flourishing – vanity, envy, brutality and insensitivity are inimical to it. In what follows, therefore, I won't challenge the misanthrope's lists of failings and virtues. Nor, at any rate until the final chapter, shall I argue for any one conception of the good life among the several to which recognition of these failings and virtues is integral.

Finally, a reminder of the misanthrope's target. This is not always or even primarily individual people, but humankind, human life, human society, human culture or forms of human life. The greed of a society, for example, is not reducible to that of certain greedy people. A greedy society is not the sum total of its greedy members, but one in which institutions, economic processes, ideology, education, its media and much else generate, condone and reward greed. Individuals are as much the product as the makers of a greedy society. Replace 'greedy' here by 'hypocritical', 'hubristic' or many another description of a failing and the point remains true. The misanthrope's target – society, humankind or whatever – varies, naturally enough, according to the failings that are under discussion. Context, therefore, will determine the most suitable term for the target.

A CHARGE LIST

Drawing up lists of human failings is not the popular practice it once was. The misanthrope's list is bound to remind readers of the catalogues of sins or moral violations that Christian theologians or Buddhist monks composed, often illustrated by lurid paintings of the terrible fates in hell of the damned or guilty. Unlike the authors of those texts, however, the misanthrope has no eschatological ambition, only that of an appraisal of humankind. As for what some will regard as the old-fashioned nature of cataloguing our failings, this is not something that disturbs the misanthrope, and rightly so.

A library catalogue doesn't simply list all the holdings on the shelves, but organises them into helpful categories, according to, say, literary genres, historical periods or academic subjects. Likewise, a list of human failings should lend structure to these. The charge list that follows is organised into clusters of failings.

Within each cluster are closely related failings, and each cluster hooks up, as it were, with an adjacent one. There are no sharp boundaries between the clusters, and a different catalogue, as in the case of libraries, might well employ a different classification. My own, I hope, will strike you as at least sensible and perhaps illuminating.

To begin with, there is what might be called the hatred cluster. This includes hatred itself, malevolence, enmity, vengefulness, *Schadenfreude* (Edmund Burke's 'delight in the real misfortunes and pains of others')[1], spitefulness and mean-spiritedness. These are loosely united by the hostility towards other people or creatures that, in varying degrees, they evince. It is a cluster of vices that motivates or is manifested in some of the worst human practices – genocide, scapegoating and racial discrimination, for example.

Behaviour that impacts badly on other people need not be the expression of anything as hostile as hatred or vengefulness. The swaggering aggression of the football fan, the obscene gesturing of the drunken clubber, the window-smashing of the mob of demonstrators manifest instead the failings of what could be labelled the loutishness cluster. Boorishness, vulgarity, rudeness, yobbishness, loutishness itself . . . the list goes on of tendencies that have in common a disregard for others. The safety, sensibilities and 'space' of other people matter nothing to the rampaging mob or the swearing lout.

The behaviour of louts and yobs is often and rightly described as mindless. And 'mindlessness', as the name for a culpable lack of attention and consideration, is a good label for a further cluster of failings. This will include carelessness, negligence and insensitivity. Special mention, perhaps, should be made of insensitivity to serious and unobvious beauty – the beauty that, unlike mere prettiness, is significant and requires effort, openness and the overcoming of prejudice to discern. As this example shows, the cluster should include various failings that encourage or reinforce mindlessness: intellectual laziness, prejudice and rigidity of outlook. Each of these obstructs a clear, open and responsive attention to the world and to the needs and goods of creatures, including one's self.

Mindlessness need not always be 'sheer'. It may be motivated, a strategy in effect for avoidance of seeing things as they are. When this is so, mindlessness is then adjacent to a further cluster of failings, the bad faith cluster. Towards one end of the spectrum of these failings are self-deceit, wilful ignorance and a proneness to be 'in denial'. Here, the victim of a person's bad faith is that same person. Towards the other end are the deceitfulness, insincerity and hypocrisy that are displayed in infidelity, betrayal, lying, treachery and sanctimonious piety. Here, the direct victims of bad faith are the people who have placed trust in, or simply relied on, the good faith and candour of the guilty person, group or institution.

One such victim, according to his own words, was Molière's misanthrope, Alceste, whose 'intention to break with all mankind' was primarily due to the flattery, deceit and betrayal that he found all around him.[2] While Molière concentrated on bad faith, it was an adjacent cluster of failings that was the focus, a century later, of Rousseau. The vanity cluster is adjacent to bad faith since vanity and its relatives typically require wilful ignorance or self-deluded denial of one's weaknesses, limitations and dependence on fortune. In this cluster, we find vanity in the sense of Rousseau's *amour-propre* ('setting greater store by oneself than by anyone else'), already encountered in Chapter 3, but also vanity in the more vernacular senses of conceit, hubris and narcissism.

We find here as well such vices as envy, self-pity and resentment at the success of others, all of which feed on a person's conviction that he or she is more deserving than others. Ingratitude, too, can be inspired by vanity. Why, the ingrate wonders, should he give thanks for what was, after all, only his rightful reward? Nor, finally, are vices of vanity unrelated to the vanity dwelt on in the book of *Ecclesiastes*. Vanity, in this sense, is the fate or condition of human life: 'all is vanity', goes the famous refrain, a 'chasing after wind' (2.11). One reason our lives are a fruitless chase, and that 'nothing is gained under the sun' (2.11), is that we have too high an opinion of our capacities, such as the ability to know the truth of things, and a corresponding reluctance to accept our 'portion in life' (9.9).

For Rousseau, we saw, *amour-propre* is not just one more evil, but 'the trigger of all the evil men do'. While it is tempting to pick upon a single failing as a sort of Ur-vice, responsible for all our other failings, it is wiser to follow the Buddhists in their emphasis on the 'dependent origination' of failings, vices and indeed everything. We should, that is, acknowledge the complex ways in which different failings reinforce and feed one another. Vanity, say, encourages envy of someone; this inspires a jealousy that modulates into a resentment that turns into enmity towards this person. Or, maybe it was emerging hatred that fed someone's sense of superiority over another person, which then encouraged envy of the person's success . . . and so on, eventually confirming and magnifying the original hatred. Here there is a circular chain of failings, without any one link as the start of the chain.

But even Buddhists give pride of place to one vice, the 'unwholesome root' of craving or greed, 'the chief root of suffering'.[3] (The other two roots are hatred and delusion.) So, let's refer to the greed cluster of human failings. Craving and greed, here, should not be envisaged, primarily, as the kind that seizes a very hungry or thirsty person, impelling him to grab too many sandwiches or glasses of wine. There is a self-referential aspect to the failings of craving and greed. The craving person is in the grip of a self-centred desire for a future state of him- or herself. Money, fame, applause, professional success are craved because, it's believed, these will secure self-satisfaction. This is why, perhaps, Buddhists refer to the craving, not for sensory pleasures, but for 'existence' as the worst and most recalcitrant kind. The greedy person is preoccupied with how he or she will *be*, how best to procure what will satisfy the demands of the ego.

The greed cluster will include, of course, what the medievals called concupiscence and cupidity. The concupiscent man is not one, simply, who is easily sexually aroused by women, but one who needs to 'have' them. Not the least of Don Juan's pleasures was to hear the roll-call of his conquests. It goes without saying that concupiscence – unrestrained desire for sexual conquest in particular – is responsible for much of the suffering and indignity that is inflicted, sometimes violently, on the victims of greed.

An important reason why Buddhist and Christian writers regard greed as especially inimical to the good life is that it is destructive of the calm, prudence and equanimity that are necessary to reflective cultivation of such a life. As the Buddha drily puts it, wisdom cannot be taught or learned by someone 'affected by greed'.[4] Craving and greed give rise to frenzy, rage and loss of self-control, and hence – in another illustration of 'dependent origination' – to the cluster of failings with which I began, hatred and resentment of those who stand in the way. Greed, as suggested earlier, is also a good example of a failing of which, not only individuals, but groups, institutions or whole societies may be guilty. One reason for this is precisely because collective bodies, too, can succumb to frenzy and rage, lose discipline and reason, in pursuit of what they crave – be it *Lebensraum*, the humiliation of enemies, wealth or entry into paradise. Not just you or I, but whole cultures may, as the Buddha taught, be 'burning', with the 'fire of craving and hatred'.[5]

Here, then, are clusters of human failings that the misanthrope has collected together in support of a negative moral verdict on humankind. There is no pretence that these failings have to be organised in just this way, nor that the failings identified are exhaustive. One can imagine, for example, another cluster that would include weakness of the will, cowardice and craven servility. Certainly, too, within each cluster on the charge list, it is easy to add further items. A depressing way of spending a few hours is to take some of the failings I have mentioned, look up their names in a good thesaurus and write down the names of related failings that you'll find listed there. You'll find there are a great many of them. But the misanthrope, in gathering a reasonably large number of our failings into a few manageable clusters, has done as much as is necessary in order to proceed with the broadly moral comparison of humans with animals. Or rather, almost enough, for there are a couple of things about these failings that first need emphasising.

UBIQUITY AND ENTRENCHMENT

It's important to the misanthrope for us to appreciate that the failings and vices on the charge sheet are not occasional or parochial features of human existence. Rather, they are ubiquitous and pervasive in human life, at least as we are familiar with it in modern times. Nor, the misanthrope will emphasise, are these failings casual or superficial features of life. Instead, they are well entrenched in it.

One reason the misanthrope emphasises the breadth and depth of human failings is that, these days, this is rarely done. Mary Midgley's remark that 'man has always been unwilling to admit his own ferocity' is surely true, as well, of many other failings.[6] It is not, perhaps, surprising that they are now dwelt upon less than they were in an age of greater eschatological concern. The Buddhist and medieval Christian catalogues of our sins and wrongs, mentioned earlier, were indispensable for people convinced that transgression would condemn them to hell or an unwelcome rebirth. But this cannot be the whole explanation. La Rochefoucauld, Molière, Voltaire, Jonathan Swift, Alexander Pope and many other seventeenth- and eighteenth-century chroniclers of human failings were not concerned with the bearing of these on people's fates after death.

To be sure, these misanthropically inclined authors identify several failings that themselves tend to obstruct honest appreciation of our vices. Mary Midgley's remark on an unwillingness to admit human ferocity indicates the role of wilful ignorance and being 'in denial' in blinding people to these failings.[6] But wilful ignorance is not the sole culprit. Hypocrisy plays its part, as does a kind of scapegoating, a pretence that it is just a few, especially bad people in whom human failings are concentrated. Vices like these conveniently serve to protect our failings at large against exposure and scrutiny.

However, we need as well to consider some characteristic tendencies of our own times to understand the current, relative silence about the breadth and depth of human failings. Some of these tendencies are fashions in contemporary moral thinking. We already noted, in Chapter 1, the contemporary focus among moral philosophers on issues of rights, justice and individual autonomy. The effect of this is to shrink the range of human failings to a small group: discrimination, violation of rights and unwarranted interference with other people's choices. It is a focus that is reflected, at the popular level, by an exhortation to 'do your own thing' provided this does not prevent others doing their own thing.

In this climate of moral thought, the idea of the good life, its virtues and the failings and vices that threaten it, becomes recessive or marginal. A person's conception of the good life gets treated as just one of those 'opinions' or 'choices' that liberal people will duly take note of and try to respect, but not as something that has moral authority. This, at any rate, is the rhetoric of our times. In practice, it is difficult to believe there are many people who regard, as being just an opinion, a conception of the good life on which self-deception, self-pity, hypocrisy, vanity and envy count as failings. These are qualities that almost no one could hope that a son or daughter would grow up to acquire. This is so even though they are failings that normally do not impinge upon the rights and autonomy of other people. Nor, surely, do many of us seriously think that the only thing wrong with greed, hatred and mindlessness is that they may lead to obstruction of the choices of other people or to violation of their rights. These would be failings on the part of a social isolate as much as on that of a socialite.

Another tendency of our times that occludes recognition of the extent and entrenchment of human failings is its mood of sunny optimism about what, deep down, we are like. Admittedly, there is plenty of doomsday talk about global warming and other threats that are placed at the door of humankind. It is striking, however, how often those who issue such warnings quickly pin the blame on a few individuals or institutions (multi-nationals, oil companies or whatever).

This optimism contrasts with a darker perception of humankind that prevailed until relatively modern times. Buddhists and medieval Christians, having identified our failings, were pessimistic about the chances of liberation or redemption. The Christian path to redemption is steep, hard and stony and the great majority of us will fail to reach the end. The Buddhist path to liberation is equally demanding, and takes countless lifetimes to climb. Today, however, in highly developed countries at least, it is a sunnier assessment of our potential that has been inherited. European Enlightenment, with its confidence in social and moral progress, has bequeathed to the mood of our times the conviction that, with the removal of certain obstacles – religious extremism, outdated institutions, prejudice, poverty – the true moral potential of humankind will be realised.

Here is not the place to discuss whether there has been and will be moral progress. For one thing, it is a discussion to which a matter not yet addressed – our treatment of animals – is relevant. The present point is to recognise the contemporary prevalence of what Alain de Botton nicely dubs 'boosterishness', a sort of buttering-up of people to make them 'more cheerful' about themselves.[7] People are encouraged to feel that, deep down, they are good. Consider, for example, how common it has become for a person accused of, say, racist remarks to apologise but then immediately add 'That's not the person I am: that wasn't the real me talking'. The boosterish attitude both reflects and reinforces what another writer calls the 'non-judgementalism' of our times, the refusal to hold people accountable for their irresponsibility and the damage this does to the lives of others.[8]

These attitudes belong to the wider optimistic view that failings owe to especially unfavourable conditions and hence, in the final analysis, are not really our failings at all. This is a view that is the reverse of one that informed social and political philosophy for many centuries. For Laozi, Machiavelli and Hobbes, for example, the truth is rather that goodness and the virtues require especially favourable conditions – the kind of conditions that their own proposals were intended to create. Virtue, the idea might be, can only flourish in the small, simple agrarian communities of which the *Daodejing* speaks.[9] Or, as Hobbes argued, people will only behave well in a society whose powerful sovereign imposes sanctions that make wrong-doing unprofitable and irrational. And all of them were aware how delicate, fragile and in need of constant vigilance these conditions are. For these thinkers, as for one present-day political philosopher of a misanthropic bent, 'being good is good luck'.[10]

What all these realists recognised is the fragility of goodness, its dependence on fair weather, on suitable conditions whose stability and perdurance cannot be relied on. When these conditions do atrophy, the results can be dreadful and the worst human failings manifest themselves. Think, for instance, of the genocidal frenzy of mobs and gangs in civil wars that begin when people can no longer trust the law, the army and other organs of political authority to protect them. Nobody, it is interesting to note, refers to the fragility of badness.

I said just now that today's boosterish optimism is heir to European Enlightenment, but in fact it exceeds anything subscribed to even by those eighteenth-century thinkers who are thought of as optimists. David Hume and Adam Smith, for example, were optimists in the sense that they rejected the philosophical egoist's claim that people only ever act out of selfish motives. They thought, too, that people are rational enough to develop sensible political and economic arrangements that favour cooperation and mutual regard. But they knew that the stability of these arrangements was not guaranteed, and knew too that benevolence and other 'social passions' were delicate plants that needed protection and nurturing. For Smith, employing a different metaphor, there exists only a 'feeble spark of benevolence . . . in the human heart', incapable of 'counteracting the strongest impulses of self-love'.[11] For Hume, likewise, sentiments like benevolence are 'ever so weak', in contrast with the 'extensive energy' of self-love.[12]

In the view of the two Scotsmen – and recall they were counted among the optimists of their times – today's sunny and lazy optimism would have perfectly illustrated what one of them noted as people's 'much greater propensity to overvalue themselves than undervalue themselves'.[13] To return to the horticultural metaphor, they knew that our failings are entrenched in human life and are not, like thinly rooted weeds, superficial aspects of our lives that come from elsewhere, do not belong there, and are easily removed by changing the conditions in which they thrive.

At the beginning of this chapter, I said that the misanthrope would argue that our failings are not only ubiquitous and entrenched, but distinctively human. It is to this last claim I turn in the following chapter. It's time to re-introduce the animals.

NOTES

1 Edmund Burke, *A Philosophical Enquiry into the Origin of Our Ideas of the Sublime and Beautiful*, Oxford: Oxford University Press, 1990, p. 42.

2 Molière, *The Misanthrope*, see n. 4 to Chapter 1.

3 Nyanatiloka, *Buddhist Dictionary*, Kandy: Buddhist Publication Society, 1997, p. 207.

4 In the Buddha's Words: An Anthology of Discourses from the Pāli Canon, ed. Bhikkhu Bodhi, Boston: Wisdom Publications, 2005, p. 99.

5 Ibid., p. 346.

6 Mary Midgley, Beast and Man, London: Penguin, 1980, p. 31.

7 Alain de Botton, in Do Humankind's Best Days Lie Ahead?: Munk Debate 2015, London: OneWorld, 2016, p. 13.

8 Theodore Dalrymple, 'Of Evil and Empathy', in his Anything Goes: The Death of Honesty, London: Monday Books (Kindle ed.), 2011.

9 See Hans-Georg Moeller (tr.), Daodejing: A Complete Translation and Commentary, Chicago: Open Court, 2007, especially Chapter 80.

10 John Gray, Straw Dogs: Thoughts on Humans and Other Animals, London: Granta, 2003, p. 104.

11 Adam Smith, The Theory of Moral Sentiments, Indianapolis, IN: Liberty Classics, 1976, p. 136.

12 David Hume, An Inquiry Concerning the Principles of Morals, Indianapolis, IN: Bobbs-Merrill, 1957, p. 92.

13 Ibid., p. 86.

5

ANIMAL VICES AND VIRTUES

In this chapter, the misanthrope finally undertakes the broadly moral comparison of human with animal lives. After considering whether animals can have failings and vices, the misanthrope argues that, even if they cannot, this does not impugn the comparison, nor does it imply that animals are without virtues.

ANIMAL VICES?

Montaigne wrote that, unlike animals, 'we have been allotted . . . ambition, greed, jealousy, envy, . . . untameable appetites, war, lies, disloyalty [and] backbiting'.[1] The misanthrope happily accepts that human life is stained by all these failings and more, but should it also be accepted that they are unique to humankind? They are, according to the misanthrope, *distinctive* of humankind, but this term is ambiguous. When we refer to a feature distinctive of a style of architecture, we might mean it is unique to this style. But we might intend something weaker: the feature is perhaps found in other styles, but it is not typical or characteristic of them. Only in the style in question is it integral and salient.

Misanthropes will defend the claim that the broadly moral failings are uniquely human, but it is not a claim that they will go to the wall for. Distinctiveness in the weaker sense is sufficient to support the misanthropic verdict on humankind. The discovery in a remote jungle of some animals that displayed cruelty and jealousy would not affect this verdict, and nor would the claim that members of one or two already familiar species occasionally display these. The misanthrope's aim, through comparing human with animal lives, is to continue with the exposure of the extent and depth of our failings and vices. That a few animals might sometimes exhibit some of these no more invalidates this aim than the occasional presence of a certain feature in other architectural styles contradicts the claim that it is distinctive only of one style.

We can certainly be very confident that many failings, at least, are unique to humankind – megalomania, self-deception, over-ambition and disloyalty, for example. This is not because animals – outside of myth and fable – have confronted these vices and heroically expelled them. Montaigne hints at the right explanation when he remarks that the vices are the price we pay for 'our fair, discursive reason and our capacity to judge and know'.[2] What Montaigne is driving at is that animals are without those fundamental features of human existence, identified in Chapter 3, that are presupposed by many, if not all, of our failings. For example, a sense of a self that extends into the past and future is a precondition for vengefulness, self-deception and hubris. But in the case of some other vices, including greed, cruelty and deceitfulness, the matter may be less clear. Certainly, ethologists have attributed these to some species of animals. Before considering the main response to such attributions, a few preliminary comments will help to draw some of their sting.

First, the number of species to which these failings get attributed is very modest. Domestic cats, chimpanzees, corvids . . . a few others. Animal species whose members allegedly deceive their fellow members, for example, belong to a small and 'exclusive club'.[3] When they do engage in deception, moreover, this is for pressing reasons: to protect a cache of food when starvation threatens, say. Human beings, as we know, require rather less justification. Second, animal behaviour that prompts attributions of failings is not the common, familiar phenomenon that permeates human life. Jane Goodall was surprised and shocked when, despite her years of experience, she first observed the brutal killings by raiding chimpanzees of animals that had once belonged with them in the same community.[4]

Goodall writes of her shock in a book subtitled 'The Living Link Between "Man" and "Beast"', and since it is apes that furnish most examples of animal vices, what her subtitle indicates deserves comment. Nietzsche remarked that apes 'devise cruelties' and thereby 'anticipate man and are, as it were, his "prelude"'.[5] Given the evolutionary and genetic closeness of humans and apes, it is unsurprising if simian behaviour anticipates some of the practices that humans engage in. But it was precisely because apes are a 'prelude' to human beings that, as was noted in Chapter 2, the misanthrope does not focus on them when comparing humans and animal lives. They do not provide the degree of contrast – the bringing into relief of human ways – that the misanthrope wants from the comparison. They are, as Nietzsche would put it, 'all-too-human'.

Goodall's own guess as to why the chimpanzees could become so lethally aggressive was the effect on them of human interventions in their life. Their behaviour was therefore not typical, but aberrant. This is a controversial claim.[6] Less contested, however, should be a similar point about the alleged vices of domesticated animals. To take the favourite example, the supposed torture that cats inflict on the mice and birds they catch almost certainly shows that, in the 'cultural context' of their home, they – unlike their wild cousins – are not 'entirely sure what to do with their prey'.[7] Eat it? Give it to someone in hope of a reward? Ignore it? From their owners, they usually only get mixed signals, a treat if they bring in a rat, a smack if it's a robin.

Piecing these comments together, even if some human failings are shared by some animals, they are not present in anything like the number, or with anything like the ubiquity, salience and pervasiveness that they are in human life. They are not, in short, distinctive of – typical of and integral to – animal life.

But should it even be conceded that these failings are found among animals at all? One expert on dogs writes that while 'it seems plausible that dogs feel something that we would label "jealousy"', this may be 'little more complex than a feeling of anxiety'. Nothing suggests that a dog become 'obsessively jealous' of another dog that shares the family home, or experiences jealousy by recollecting earlier occasions involving this other dog.[8] While it is not exactly a mistake to call the dog jealous, the term does not have the full, pejorative sense it typically does when applied to people. Lacking a sense of itself as extending back into the past, the dog's jealousy is of an attenuated kind that runs no risk of becoming consuming or obsessive. And crucially, it is questionable if this attenuated jealousy is a failing or vice. The dog's spasmodic feelings of jealousy when another dog is petted do not eat away at him, spoil his daily social life or build up into dangerous resentment.

The point here is a general one. Many terms for failings are sometimes used without critical force, without any intention to condemn or censure. A lazy swim, a tennis player's deceptive serve, being greedy for information, the cruel victory of a cricket team . . . none of these illustrate failings. Perhaps the uses of the terms should be counted as figurative, but the border between literal use and figurative use is fuzzy. We need to allow, as in the case of 'jealousy', for uses in the no man's land between the two – uses that, crucially, are stripped of critical or pejorative force.

Let's briefly consider, in the light of this, whether the greed, deception and cruelty attributed to animals are ever the failings they are with human beings. Greed, in fact, has already been dealt with when, in Chapter 4, we noted the Buddhist elevation of greed or craving to pride of place among the vices. Greed – the vice of greed, that is, as described in that chapter – is not the stuffing down of food by a ravenous man or wolf, but desire for future states of one's self. Greed, as a failing, is possible only for creatures whose lives are an 'issue' for them, who have a conception of what they want to become – rich, honoured, sexually successful or whatever. Animals are not such creatures.

Deception, as a failing, is more complex than simply fooling people. We don't condemn the illusionist who deceives the audience as to the whereabouts of the rabbit. This is because there is no breach of trust, no violation of what anyone legitimately expects from an illusionist's show. Trust and legitimate expectation presuppose a form of social life, in which rules, conventions and sanctions shape both how people will act and how they expect others to act. This is a form of life unavailable to creatures without an understanding of past commitments and future obligations. The crow that pretends to bury some food is only deceiving the watching birds in the sense that the illusionist deceives an audience. No rules are broken, no trust breached.

Informed observers of stomach-churning animal practices are reluctant to describe these, without qualification, as cruel. Goodall, appalled as she was by cannibalistic chimpanzee attacks, nevertheless insisted that 'only humans . . . are capable of *deliberate* cruelty', for only they have 'the intention of causing pain and suffering'.[9] Konrad Lorenz refers to that 'most terrible predator', the water-shrew, as 'innocently-cruel' – unlike a human being who inflicts pain on 'creatures that he hunts for pleasure and not for food'.[10] Cruelty is a complex notion, involving the idea of intentionally inflicting unnecessary harm, suffering or pain and for reasons (like pleasure) other than the good of the creature it is inflicted on.[11] (Spanish Inquisitors, who thought confessions on the rack were essential to the victims' salvation, could reasonably deny, from their perspective, that they were being any more cruel than the surgeons of the period.) Creatures incapable of understanding this idea – creatures without a reflective moral sense – are at most 'innocently-cruel'. The 'terrible' water-shrew hurts its prey, but to feed its young, not for fun, and it does so without any conception of what it is to cause unnecessary harm to another being.

If these remarks are well taken, animals are free of the broadly moral failings distinctive of human life. At the very least, if there are animal vices then these do not compare in number, extent and entrenchment with our own. The misanthrope recognises, however, that this conclusion is insufficient to show that the comparison between humans and animals supports the misanthropic verdict. There is a further matter that needs attention.

HUMAN VIRTUES

This further matter is the virtues of humankind. An elephant, in one of Vikram Seth's engaging set of *Beastly Tales*, explains to his animal audience the nature of Man. A human being, the elephant reflects, is a creature that is both 'mild and vicious', 'loving and brutal', 'sane and mad'. In human nature, 'the good is as puzzling as the bad'.[12] The elephant duly mentions some human failings, but rightly refers to virtues that contrast with them. Is it not invidious of the misanthrope to compare us with animals by attending only to our failings? If animals are without vice, it will be said, then presumably they are also without virtue. But in that case, what prevents the misanthrope's critic from placing us *above* animals on account of our virtues? This, perhaps, was Konrad Lorenz's point when, despite his harsh remarks on humankind and warm admiration for animals, he denounces as 'sheer blasphemy' the thought that 'animals are better than men'.[13]

Rather than reverse the misanthrope's verdict, however, the critic might do better to argue that, since animals are neither vicious nor virtuous, moral comparison between them and creatures who are both – ourselves, that is – is illegitimate, senseless even. The critic is assuming here that if animals have no vices then they have no virtues either. This is an assumption that misanthropes will shortly challenge. Before that, however, they will argue that, *even* if this assumption is correct, that doesn't affect the legitimacy of the moral comparison.

There's one argument, however, the misanthrope won't use even though, historically, it has been popular among some misanthropic thinkers, those that have been labelled 'psychological egotists'. Their claim is that human beings have no virtues, only vices. Such might be the implication of Thomas Hobbes's statements that 'of all voluntary acts, the object to every man is his own good' and that a man's good is simply whatever he has an 'appetite or desire' for.[14] Virtue, it seems, is an illusion, selfishness with a veil. But this is not a view misanthropes need to take. Indeed, they may agree with Bishop Butler and David Hume that it is paradoxical to hold that people never act out of compassion or loyalty, say, but only for self-satisfaction.[15] For how, they asked, could people find satisfaction in what they do unless the compassion or loyalty is genuine? I won't feel good about myself if feeling good about myself is my sole motive.

The misanthrope's response to the critic is not, then, to deny that human beings can be virtuous. Rather it is to argue that it is better to be a creature who is neither vicious or virtuous than one, like ourselves, who is both. Attitudes to vice and virtue respectively are not symmetrical. Vices and other failings disturb us more than virtues please us, and more weight is placed on resisting or suppressing our vices than on cultivating virtues. There are instructive parallels here with asymmetries in the cases of pain and pleasure and of harm and benefit. Generally, people are significantly more concerned to avoid or reduce pain and harm than to gain pleasures and benefits.[16]

The asymmetry between vice and virtue explains several features of the moral landscape. It explains, for example, why the moral codes promulgated in the great religions consist predominantly in prohibitions, in censuring vices, rather than in exhortations to virtue. Eight out of the Ten Commandments tell us what not to engage in – lust, envy, dishonesty and so on; only one commands us to exercise a virtue, that of honouring parents. The Five Precepts that form the core of Buddhist moral regulation are all prohibitions – against harming creatures, lying and so on. Second, it explains why many virtues are, so to speak, only reactive, since they amount to little more than resistance to the corresponding vices. Temperance, for instance, is valued because temperate people are not greedy. Greed, by contrast, is not condemned *because* it is the absence of temperance.

Someone who doubts the existence of the asymmetry should consult the intuitions most of us have on whether the virtues of a person – or institution or society – can compensate for their vices and failings. The hypocrite and traitor are remembered for their hypocrisy and treachery, not for the patience and generosity they may also have displayed. It would be a joke, or gross moral insensitivity, to defend a sadistic torturer on the ground that he demonstrated impartiality and humility when at his work.

Examples like these indicate a reason for placing less weight on the virtues. This is their fragility. By this I mean the ease with which many virtues may become failings, tipping over into helpmates of the vices. Kant pointed out that the very calmness and self-control we admire in normal circumstances can make a scoundrel all the more 'dangerous' and 'abominable'.[17] Something similar could be said of the patience of the traitor, the dedication of the torturer or the courage of the suicide bomber. There is, by contrast, no parallel fragility of vice.

Material greed and hatred do not run the risk of turning into helpmates of the virtues.

It is true that, despite the asymmetry, if human life were saturated with virtue and stained only by occasional failings, then the misanthrope's verdict might be overturned. This seems to be the view of Stephen Jay Gould, who wrote of the 'billion tiny acts of kindness' done by millions of people as an overwhelmingly 'powerful counterweight' to 'rare acts of depravity'.[18] 'Faith' might be a better word than 'view', for it would be absurdly impractical to tot up the numbers of vicious and virtuous deeds performed in the history of humankind. More importantly, it is a view that will seem strange to anyone impressed by the misanthrope's long charge list of human failings. Acts of depravity may be relatively rare, but other acts that manifest our failings certainly aren't. The number of these failings, and their ubiquity and entrenchment, indeed require a 'powerful counterweight' if, given the greater weight placed on vice than on virtue, they are not to yield the misanthrope's verdict.

I see no reason to think this counterweight is available. Vikram Seth's elephant, despite an attempt to balance the failings and virtues of human beings, is forced to conclude that humankind is a 'mess', at the 'sticky centre' of which is an 'uneasy selfishness' – a self-centredness testified to by all or most of our failings. The misanthrope agrees.

So, better to be without either virtue or vice than to engage in both. Better still, of course, is to have virtues but no vices or failings. This is what the misanthrope will now argue is the condition of many animals.

ANIMAL VIRTUES

Some people are reluctant to think that animals can be virtuous, and not simply out of a general fear of being accused of anthropomorphism. They have the understandable worry that many virtues, at least, presuppose distinctively human forms of life. Humility, for example, is confined to beings that can compare themselves with one another and recognise their achievements and limitations. This worry is compounded by the claim, defended a few pages back, that animals do not have vices. Won't the reasons given for that claim also apply to virtues?

Before arguing for the existence of animal virtues, here are a few remarks that may loosen the conviction that if animals are vice-less they must be virtue-less too. We should note, for a start, that in many world religions there are figures that are deemed to be entirely virtuous, without any accompanying failings. Not only the founding figures of these religions – the Buddha, Mahavira and Jesus, for example – but a host of saints, bodhisattvas and holy men or women are venerated or worshipped because of this. Second, there's a parallel between crediting animals with virtue but not vice and the idea, subscribed to by many thinkers, that there is beauty in the natural world, but no ugliness. The Stoic Roman Emperor, Marcus Aurelius, applied this idea to our appreciation of animals. To find a cheetah or even a hyena beautiful, we don't need to find other creatures ugly. Once we set aside our uneducated aversions and see the hyena for what it is, we recognise its beauty.[19] Why shouldn't something analogous obtain in the case of an animal's goodness? If it does, there is nothing paradoxical in Konrad Lorenz's remark that a wild animal's 'urges' can only be 'good'.[20]

Finally, there is some parallel too with our attitudes towards the emotions of young children. It is not just sentimentality or maternal pride that makes a mother willing to describe her child as loving and affectionate, while refusing to describe it as hateful, scornful or malevolent. Young children are too innocent to experience such vicious feelings – innocent, not in the sense of 'not guilty', but of being as yet uncorrupted by a complex adult world that provides scope and material for hatred, scorn, malevolence and the rest of our failings.

The vices presuppose a loss of innocence in a way that at least some virtues do not. The innocence of a being – its distance from the machinations, complications and temptations of adult human life – dissolves the inclination to speak of it in the language of vices and failings. It does not similarly dissolve an urge to do so in the vocabulary of virtue. And this is as true in the case of animals as that of young children. Drawing on his study of the relationships between animals and North American hunter-gatherers, a distinguished anthropologist writes that 'we see animals as innocent . . . untainted by the ambiguities, distractions and complexities' of human thought, speech and society. Lions, he reminds us, 'do not lie'. Because of this innocence, animals 'arouse in us a form of gentle sympathy'[21] – as do young children and 'holy fools', and for the same reason.

It belongs to this 'gentle sympathy' to discern goodness in the behaviour of animals. I watch two crows on a wall outside my study window, tenderly nuzzling and preening each other, and I am moved by this. My affection and esteem for crows is confirmed. When, yesterday, I saw another couple of crows squabbling over some carrion, this sympathy was not damaged. Both the nuzzling and the squabbling, of course, are entirely natural – innocent, if you like. But while the natural intimacy of the birds does nothing to exclude a sense of their goodness, the naturalness of the aggression of hungry birds does erode a sense of their badness. You might reply that our feeling of gentle sympathy and our inclination to use the language of virtue is neither here nor there. Feelings and inclinations are a subjective thing; what is wanted is objective assessment of the characteristics of animals. But, in the final analysis, the question whether animals exercise compassion and equanimity, say, is not separable from how natural and compelling we find it to apply the terms for these virtues. Natural and compelling, that is, in the light of a proper perception – free from prejudice, hubris and fantasy – of the animals for what they are. That animal lives are 'morally inflected', as one philosopher puts it, depends not just on the bare facts of animal behaviour, but on our mindful engagement with and our 'complex responses' to animals.[22]

But which virtues can be attributed to animals? Not the merely reactive ones, referred to earlier, that are little more than the absence of corresponding vices. Nor those that clearly presuppose, as do the vices, such fundamental features of human life as a reflective moral sense, *amour-propre*, and being an 'issue' for one's self. This still leaves many candidate virtues. I propose that dogs and other animals manifest at least the virtues of compassion, loyalty and gratitude, equanimity and spontaneity, but not such corresponding failings as callousness or treachery. Let's briefly consider these.

An elephant protects and helps the injured calf of a dead sister. She displays concern and compassion. But when she walks straight past another injured animal, she is not being callous or hard of heart. Hardness of heart requires the recognition that sympathy is expected and called for. A crow is loyal to its partner, caring for her, responding to her needs, protecting her against danger. But another crow that leaves its mate is not guilty of disloyalty. For it has not made the commitments, and lacks a sense of how the past engenders obligations, that disloyalty and betrayal presuppose.

A dog shows gratitude when he is helped to find a bone or has a wound patched up. But he does not display ingratitude when he leaves, without a backward glance, the house of someone who has been looking after him for the day. In his moving essay, 'Death of a Dog', the philosopher Rush Rhees wrote that his dog, Danny, 'never showed ingratitude or harboured resentment'.[23] He meant, I think, that Danny *couldn't* show ingratitude. Gratitude is simple, innocent, natural, unreflective. The ingrate, by contrast, must recognise that the thanks he or she refuses to give are deserved, and this is not something Danny could do.

A wolf shows equanimity when, although grieving, it accepts without sentimentality and demur the death of its mate. But its shows no resentment or vengefulness towards the hunter who shot it. For the wolf, perhaps, the hunter is to blame only in the sense that a harsh winter is to blame for the death of a cub. Crows and many other creatures are rightly credited with spontaneity – with, that is, alert, mindful attention and responsiveness to the world. But animals that are less spontaneous are not therefore guilty of the prejudices, rigid conventions or wilful ignorance that are destructive of spontaneity and mindfulness in human affairs. Only people can will their ignorance or go along with the prejudices of their fellows.

In the case of each of these animal virtues, a similar point is being made. We discern virtues in the simple, unreflective, natural behaviour of the animals. We cannot similarly discern failings and vices in their behaviour, for these are grounded in dimensions of a kind of life that is unique to us. Here is another important asymmetry, to add to the one discussed on p. 67, in our attitudes to virtues and vices respectively. If this is right, there is good reason to applaud the following tribute to dogs: 'In dogs, we've bred the people we wish we could be: loyal, hardworking, watchful, fiercely protective, intuitive, sensitive, affectionate, helpful to those in need'.[24] It's a tribute of a kind appropriate to other types of animal as well.

Some biologists and zoologists want to go further in the attribution of virtues to animals. In particular, they claim that some animals – apes, crows, dogs and others – have a sense of justice, that they have an understanding of fairness and equity.[25] The claim is made, typically, on the basis of highly artificial experimental situations in which, for instance, a monkey's level of agitation is measured when it sees another monkey getting a grape instead of the cucumber that they have both been contentedly receiving so far. It's often made, too, with the peculiar proviso that an animal's unjust, unfair behaviour is nothing to criticise it for. Peculiar, since a full-blooded understanding of what it is to act unjustly surely contains an appreciation of that which is wrong.

The problem with the claim that animals can demonstrate the virtues of justice and fairness is that, if they can do this, they can also display the failings of injustice and unfairness. But this contradicts what was argued earlier – that no such failings can be attributed to animals. These virtues and vices alike presuppose a grasp of rules, entitlements and deserts, and more generally participation in forms of life distinctive of human existence.

It is uncompelling to suppose that any animals have this grasp. Something more primitive – more innocent, as it were – than an offended sense of justice is at work when an animal gets agitated at 'unfair' treatment; 'disproportion aversion', as it's been called, or simply the perception of a disturbing change in a familiar pattern of distribution.[26] The idea that the animal has the capacity to reflect on its entitlements and on what count as violations of a norm is, if earlier arguments are right, implausible. I am agreeing, in effect, that for animals to act virtuously it is unnecessary, as Mark Rowlands puts it, that they 'adopt an impartial perspective of the sort required for a sense of justice'. All that is required is that we are able to discern in the animal's actions and gestures the expression of various 'moral emotions', as he calls them, such as compassion and gratitude.[27]

The misanthrope's comparison of human and animal life has vindicated the conclusion that – in contrast with Hume's judgement – the comparison is favourable to the animals. Montaigne and others were right to think that a broadly moral contrast with animals would bring our failings into relief and compel a lower estimate of humankind than most people are liable to make. The misanthrope has exposed the range and depth of human failings and argued that animals by contrast are without vices. It was conceded that men and women of course exercise virtues, but it was also shown that it is better to be a creature without either virtues or vices than to be one with both. Best of all is to have only the virtues and this, it was urged, is precisely what some animals have.

CODA: BEAUTY AND VIRTUE

I want to return to the analogy, on p. 69, between virtues without corresponding vices and natural beauty without corresponding ugliness. In fact, there is more than an analogy here, and to understand this will confirm and inflect the appreciation of animal virtues. A so-called 'positive' aesthetics of nature was familiar in ancient teachings – Stoic, Neo-Platonic and Buddhist – that treat ugliness as an expression of evil.[28] An ugly face is one that conveys malice or brutality, while one that expresses compassion or humility is seen as beautiful by people able to transcend shallow, conventional criteria of beauty. The expression of a person's goodness in facial features, gestures and actions is precisely what enables beauty to be magnetic, to draw us to such a person.

The point applies to animals, too. The beauty we find in them is expressive of qualities that we admire as belonging to the good life, in people as well as animals – grace, courage, alertness, compassion and much else. It is no surprise that in mythology and art, beautiful animals are often emblematic of virtue. It was Holman Hunt's *The Scapegoat* that inspired John Ruskin's remark that 'the beauty of the animal form is in exact proportion to the . . . moral . . . virtue expressed by it'.[29] We know from his notebooks and fables that a great painter of animals, Leonardo da Vinci, perceived the beauty of horses, birds, dogs, cats and even insects as pointing to their virtues – generosity, humility and honesty, for example.[30]

If evil and failings are found only in humankind and its products, and not in nature, there is no ugliness in nature either. As Marcus Aurelius explained, once animals are clearly seen for what they are, with their purposes and their place in the natural order understood, it is only their beauty that can be recognised. In enjoying the beauty of animals that is expressive of their good, then, we are brought face to face with – we in effect experience – their goodness. The experience serves at once to confirm the misanthrope's confinement of vice to human beings, and as an important element in the authentic engagement, or way of being, with animals that is the topic for Chapter 9.

NOTES

1 Michel de Montaigne, *The Complete Essays*, London: Penguin, 1991, p. 541.

2 Ibid.

3 Candice Savage, *Crows*, Vancouver: Greystone, 2015, p. 91. On corvid deception, see Bernd Heinrich, *Mind of the Raven*, New York: Harper-Collins, 2006, Chapter 22.

4 Jane Goodall, *The Chimpanzee: The Living Link Between "Man" and "Beast"*, Edinburgh: Edinburgh University Press, 1992, p. 15.

5 Friedrich Nietzsche, *On the Genealogy of Morals*, in *Basic Writings of Nietzsche*, New York: Modern Library, 1968, II.6.

6 Jeffrey Masson, *Beasts: What Animals Can Teach Us about the Origins of Good and Evil*, New York: Bloomsbury, 2014, pp. 60–2.

7 Ibid., p. 187 n. 1.

8 John Bradshaw, *In Defence of Dogs*, London: Penguin, 2012, p. 252.

9 Goodall, quoted in Masson, *Beasts*, p. 59.

10 Konrad Lorenz, *King Solomon's Ring*, London: Methuen, 1961, pp. 106–7.

11 For a helpful discussion of cruelty, see David Livingstone Smith, *Less Than Human: Why Do We Demean, Enslave, and Exterminate Others?* New York: St Martin's Griffin, 2012, Chapter 7.

12 Vikram Seth, 'The Elephant and the Tragopan', in *Beastly Tales*, London: Phoenix, 1991, p. 101.

13 Lorenz, *Man Meets Dog*, London: Penguin, 1964, p. 68.

14 Thomas Hobbes, *Leviathan*, Oxford: Blackwell, 1960, pp. 32, 99.

15 Joseph Butler, *Five Sermons: A Dissertation on the Nature of Virtue*, Indianapolis, IN: Hackett, 1983, Sermon IV; David Hume, *An Inquiry*

into the Principles of Morals, Indianapolis, IN: Bobbs-Merrill, 1957, Appendix II.

16 See David Benatar and David Wasserman, Debating Procreation: Is It Wrong to Procreate?, Oxford: Oxford University Press, pp. 105ff, on these parallels.

17 Immanuel Kant, Groundwork for the Metaphysics of Morals, New York: Broadview, 2005, p. 55.

18 Quoted in Masson, Beasts, p. 150.

19 Marcus Aurelius, The Meditations, Indianapolis, IN: Hackett, 1983, Bk 3 § 2. See also David E. Cooper, 'Beauty and the Cosmos', Harvard Review of Philosophy, 19, 2013, pp. 106–17.

20 Lorenz, Man Meets Dog, p. 182.

21 Hugh Brody, The Other Side of Eden: Hunter-Gatherers, Farmers and the Shaping of the World, London: Faber & Faber, 2001, p. 290.

22 Simon Coughlan, 'Recognizing Nonhuman Morality', Between the Species, 17, 2014, p. 102.

23 Rush Rhees, Moral Questions, London: Palgrave Macmillan, 1999, p. 199.

24 Carl Safina, Beyond Words: What Animals Think, London: Souvenir, 2015, p. 238.

25 See Frans de Waal, The Age of Empathy: Nature's Lessons for a Kinder Society, London: Souvenir, 2010, Chapter 6.

26 Coughlan, 'Recognizing Nonhuman Morality', p. 98.

27 Mark Rowlands, Can Animals Be Moral? Oxford: Oxford University Press, 2015, p. 22.

28 See, for example, Marcus Aurelius, The Meditations, Book 3; Plotinus, The Enneads, London: Penguin, I.6; and David E. Cooper, 'Buddhism, Beauty and Virtue', in K. Higgins, S. Maira and S. Sikka (eds.), Artistic Visions and the Promise of Beauty, New York: Springer, 2016, pp. 125–38. On views on animal beauty in particular, see Stephen Davies, The Artful Species: Aesthetics, Art, and Evolution, Oxford: Oxford University Press, 2012, Chapter 5.

29 Quoted in Kenneth Clark, Animals and Men, London: Thames & Hudson, 1977, p. 103.

30 Leonardo da Vinci, Notebooks, Oxford: Oxford University Press, 2008.

6

TREATMENT OF ANIMALS

'BRUTALITY TO "BRUTES"'

Having compared human with animal life, attention now turns to the treatment of animals and the attitudes that inform this treatment. In this and the next chapter, I defend the misanthropic response to this treatment, a response nicely encapsulated in the words of a policeman in Louis de Bernières's factually based story of Red, a dog living in the Australian outback.

> Who'd give Red poison, for God's sake? He's everyone's pet dog. . . . The things I've seen since I was a policeman, you just wouldn't believe. I'll tell you mate, there's no animal lower than us in the whole damn world.[1]

Although the two ways of exposing the depth and breadth of human failings are different, they are connected. Someone who embarks on comparing human with animal life will soon be struck by the uniquely awful ways in which human beings treat other species. Equally, anyone who sets out to chronicle this treatment cannot ignore its implications for the comparison of humans with animals.

In this chapter the misanthrope, after a survey of humankind's criminal treatment of animals, asks about the terms in which the wrongness of this treatment should be understood. In the following chapter, the misanthrope argues that the wrong we do to animals is an especially fundamental one, not just one more wrong to add to the list. It will help to prepare for these discussions to recall and add to some misanthropic denunciations of our usage of animals.

For one philosopher we cited (p. 19), it was humankind's 'brutality to "brutes"' that, alongside 'inhumanity to humans', constituted his 'misanthropic argument' for the 'anti-natalist' conclusion that he defends. Whether or not this conclusion is accepted, it is true that the fate, at our hands, of brutes should be a main component in the misanthropic vision. For another philosopher, confirmation of his 'natural misanthropy' could be found in the 'human evil' that is distilled in animal experimentation (p. 2).

And here are some especially powerful remarks by three acclaimed authors of fiction, each of whose negative appraisal of humankind is significantly shaped by revulsion at its treatment of animals. The protagonist in a short story by Isaac Bashevis Singer refers to humankind as 'the worst transgressor of all the species', one that he can bear 'no longer to be part of'. The main reason that Herman gives for his disgust is the terrible conviction of 'man . . . that all other creatures were created merely to provide him with food, pelts, to be tormented, exterminated'. In relation to animals, he continues, all people are Nazis, and existence 'for the animals is an eternal Treblinka'.[2] The controversial Treblinka analogy, to which we'll return in Chapter 7, is repeated by Esther Costello, the central character in J.M. Coetzee's book, *The Lives of Animals*. For Esther, the treatment of animals in the modern world – above all in the food industry – is 'an enterprise of degradation, cruelty and killing' that, being 'without end, self-regenerating', 'dwarfs' in scale what happened in the Third Reich. Nearly all of us, day in day out, are, she charges, 'participants in a crime of stupefying proportions'. If, in behaving as we do towards animals, we are simply obeying 'human nature', then 'we bring down on ourselves a curse thereby'.[3]

Finally, here is a celebrated passage, mentioned at the beginning of this book, from Milan Kundera's The Unbearable Lightness of Being:

> Mankind's true moral test . . . consists of its attitude towards those who are at its mercy: animals. And in this respect mankind has suffered a fundamental debacle, a debacle so fundamental that all others follow from it.[4]

A theme common to these three works is that it is not the brute fact of animal suffering that warrants the moral censure of humankind. Causing suffering can, after all, sometimes be justified or excused. Maybe it is necessary to avert even greater suffering, or maybe it is being done out of blameless ignorance. What warrants the moral verdict, rather, is the attitudes and other failings that are responsible for the suffering and degradation of animals. Singer speaks of the hubristic conviction that humankind is 'the crown of creation'; Coetzee of the cruelty and indifference of which we are guilty; Kundera of a merciless attitude towards animals. We'll soon be adding to this list of failings, but first, in case we still need them, some reminders of the kinds of treatment of animals that invite the misanthrope's judgement on human practice and life.

ANOTHER CHARGE LIST

The aim in this section is not to compete with the many well-researched books that provide detailed, comprehensive accounts of the ills visited upon animals by human beings.[5] The purpose rather is to draw up, in a loosely organised way, a brief charge list of our treatment of animals, and to indicate features of this treatment to which the misanthrope pays special attention – the casualness, for example, with which animals are often subjected to great suffering.

As with the earlier charge list of human failings in Chapter 4, there is no single way to categorise the variety of treatment meted out to animals. A familiar way, one which I'll follow, is to consider the various walks of human life – the different kinds of human practice – in which animals, to their cost, are entangled. Cooking, entertainment, work, fashion, medicine, sport – in these and other sectors of human life, we have dealings with and make use of animals. Pack mules, beach donkeys, roasted chickens, skinned minks, dancing bears, hunted foxes, laboratory mice, poached elephants, domestic cats, jumping horses, venom-milked snakes, force-fed geese – these are just a few of the creatures, alive or dead, that are in the service of human beings, catering to their needs or desires.

The largest and most discussed kind of human practice involving animals is, of course, the eating of them. Billions of creatures each year are consumed by people, a high proportion of these raised in batteries, cages, CAFO (Concentrated Animal Feeding Operation) sites, fish farms and other installations on an industrial scale. Most of these animals lead short lives, confined and crowded together with their fellows, fed on foods that pump them up. In the words of the title of a pioneering book on factory farming, these creatures are 'animal machines', devices for the cheap and fast conversion of bodies into edible stuff.[6] In order to keep them from fighting or dying prematurely, they are debeaked, declawed or drugged up. And when it is time for them to die, they are taken, often thirsty and frightened, to places where – as we know from undercover films – their deaths are frequently painful and slow, the victims of bungled executions carried out by men with no care for them. Plenty of fish, too, have very unpleasant deaths: dragged up by trawler nets from the depths, their bladders are so inflated by gas bubbles that their stomachs burst through their mouths.

All of this is routine suffering for the billions of creatures we eat. In the case of many others, our refined taste for certain foods means that the suffering is more prolonged or intense. Geese have oily corn stuffed through funnels into their oesophagi in order to enlarge their livers. Calves are kept in total darkness, too confined and anaemic to move, so that that their flesh will be milky white and soft. Snakes are skinned alive before being chopped up; frogs have their legs ripped off before being tossed aside; live monkeys have the top of their skulls sliced off and the spoons of Chinese diners in Guangdon plunged into their brains.

It is not only for the purpose of being eaten that huge numbers of animals suffer pain, exist in appalling conditions and experience terrible deaths. People's desires to make themselves more attractive, more enviable and more sexually potent are among the other motives. Foxes and minks die slowly in rusty traps before they are skinned; crocodiles and alligators are squashed together in farms that supply the handbag industry; elephants and rhinos, sometimes still alive, have tusks or horns torn out; tigers starve to death before their bones are mixed into a 'wine' advertised as an aphrodisiac.

Some of these uses of animals – the testing on rabbits for the safety of cosmetics, for example – shade into medical ones. Imprisoned bears, sometimes over the course of twenty years, regularly have their gall bladders punctured to extract a bile wrongly reputed to cure hangovers and sore throats. Several thousand bears are subjected to this, a number tiny, however, in comparison with the millions of animals that end their days in medical laboratories. They include mice genetically programmed to develop huge cancerous tumours, rats whose spines are severed, creatures that are welded together like Siamese twins and ones used to test how much pain can be caused before the brain closes down. Monkeys have been placed in 'wells of despair', featureless metal tubes, in order to find out how soon they go insane. Dogs are given electric shocks to test how quickly they give up even trying to escape them and sink into a state of 'learned helplessness'. These experiments are sometimes defended on the grounds that the animals subjected to them are purpose bred. Bringing a creature into existence simply in order to experiment on it is legitimate apparently.

It is not, of course, only for medical purposes that animals are specially bred. So are huge numbers of pets, above all dogs. Many of these live well, but many do not. In the United States, the average pet is kept by its owners for only two years: the discarded dogs and cats are generally put down after a few desolate weeks in a pound. Discarded, too – this time by breeders – are the many dogs that fail to meet the exacting standards for pedigree animals which buyers expect. The fate of these dogs is better, perhaps, than that of many animals who do meet these standards – ones, in the case of various breeds, that can hardly breathe, whose eyes are in danger of popping out, or are subject to perpetual nervous anxiety. The figures given by organisations like the RSPCA for cruelty to pets rise inexorably each year. Even pets that are not victims of cruelty often lead miserable lives because of their owners' failure to understand their needs – dogs, for example, who suffer intense loneliness all day long during the working week. Zhuangzi's cautionary tale of the ruler who inadvertently kills a pet bird by imposing on it a luxury diet and lifestyle, instead of allowing the bird to eat 'wiggly things' and 'perch in the deep forest', deserves retelling again and again.[7]

Pets are supposed to give people pleasure, and so are the many animals that have been commandeered for purposes of entertainment. Bears have been disciplined into dancing for us; elephants, lions, tigers and seals forced into performing in the circus ring; wolves and gorillas compelled to spend their lives behind bars being stared at, sometimes laughed at, by visitors to zoos or, as some of the worst of these are now called in popular tourist destinations, animal 'sanctuaries'.

Much of the entertainment animals are made to provide is known as sport. Dogs, cockerels and other creatures are trained to fight to the death, cheered on by aficionados. A quarter of a million bulls are dispatched each year in the bull ring, many having first had their testicles squashed, their stomachs pumped with laxatives and their neck muscles severed so that they won't put up too much of a fight. Horses are bred to race, many of them being put down because of injuries they sustain, while the rest – except for a lucky few – are butchered once their racing days are over. The same destiny awaits many racing greyhounds, unless instead they are sold to laboratories.

The most enduring and popular of the blood sports are recreational hunting, shooting and fishing. Whole animal populations – American bisons, Indian elephants, European wolves – have sometimes been brought to the verge of extinction by hunters. Unlike fighting cocks or racehorses, the victims of these sports have no role to play other than to be shot or hooked, and then perhaps eaten, worn or turned into trophies on walls or in glass cases. Many of the intended victims – grouse and pheasants, for example – either die on the roads or, only wounded by the shooters, expire of their injuries in ditches and fields. Eating what they have shot or hooked is anyway not the primary purpose for most enthusiasts. Close to my home is a fishery – a place where men spend the day catching trout, removing the hook and throwing the fish back until, a few hours later, the process is repeated. I sometimes try to calculate how many times during its tormented lifetime a given fish has had a hook torn from its sensitive lip.

There are countless other creatures that are not killed for sport, though if the killing proves enjoyable, this is a bonus. In fact, they are not killed because they serve some purpose but, on the contrary, because they get in the way of various human practices, such as farming, gardening, birdwatching and outdoor dining. They are called vermin and pests. Moles are gassed, rats poisoned, foxes trapped, crows and seagulls shot. Fashion changes as to what counts as a pest. Wolves are now revered by some people as symbols of the wild rather than, as previously, portrayed as the epitome of evil in children's fiction and mercilessly hunted down. By contrast, grey squirrels in Britain, once 'cute', amusing and enterprising, have now become targets of xenophobic hostility; they allegedly drive out the 'native' red squirrels – ones, that is, which have lived in the country for somewhat longer than the greys.

Finally, mention should be made of the millions of creatures that die, often horribly, not because they are targets like vermin and pests, but because, nevertheless, they get in the way of human plans and practices. It's not just fish that are caught in nets, but dolphins and frigate birds. Whales are beached and die because they have been deafened and disorientated by the sounds of ships and submarines. The conversion of traditional English landscapes into huge monocultural fields has removed the hedges, plants and flower meadows on which many animals – bees, hedgehogs, birds – depended. Further east and also in South America, the existence in several countries of whole species – leopards, apes and so on – is threatened by forestry, jungle clearances, livestock farming, hydro projects and other interventions.

The charge list could go on . . . and on. I haven't, for instance, mentioned the suffering of animals that are still put to work for us – pack mules, say, or cart-pulling buffalos and tree-lifting elephants. But the list is long and varied enough for the misanthrope to consult when reflecting on our treatment of animals and what it shows about us.

The list is long enough, for a start, to illustrate the great variety of ways in which animals suffer at our hands. Whether through providing human beings with food, entertainment, sport, raw materials, bodies on which to experiment or domestic company, animals are subjected to pain, fear, wretched deaths, ridicule or abandonment. The list is sufficiently long, as well, to indicate the scale – the 'stupendous proportions', to recall Coetzee's words – of the criminal treatment dealt out to animals. The figures are so large that they make the head swim. It is reckoned, for example, that around 200 billion creatures a year are killed for the food they provide us with.

What is also apparent from some items on the list is the triviality of many of the alleged human benefits that accrue from the suffering and deaths of animals. 'For the sake of a little mouthful of flesh', observed Plutarch, 'we deprive a soul of the sun and the light' and its allotted life.[8] The flavour of liver paste, the look of a coat or collar, the introduction of a new hair shampoo – these are sufficient reason, it seems, to warrant force-feeding geese, trapping foxes or dripping chemicals into the eyes of rabbits. Whereas men once hunted animals to provide their families with essential food, millions of game birds are now shot in order to give pleasant days out in the open air, replete with champagne and picnic hampers, to parties of shooters.

Modern-day recreational hunting illustrates another feature of our treatment of animals – the casualness with which they are caused to suffer or die. There is no sense among today's shooters that killing creatures is anything significant, anything to question or regret. 'They aren't hunters, these men', writes Margaret Atwood, 'they have none of the patience of hunters, none of the remorse'.[9] It is with the same casualness and absence of regret that people sprinkle poison on the ground for rats to swallow, point out to the waiter which of the trussed-up lobsters they want for their lunch, toss aside the live frogs whose legs have been ripped off or send off an email to order a new batch of mice for the research laboratory.

The list displays, finally, a feature especially relevant to the misanthropic verdict on humankind – the feature, indeed, that encourages the choice of humankind, rather than individual people, as the primary target of the verdict. It is, of course, possible to pick out certain men and women as especially criminal in their maltreatment of animals – ones who place monkeys down 'wells of despair', let their pet dogs starve to death or take sadistic pleasure in using cats for target practice. But the great bulk of the misuse of animals is, as it were, institutionalised – something that infuses and is entrenched in communal, cultural and social practices.

Alice Walker writes that our crimes against nature, animals included, represent 'our worst collective behaviour'.[10] Even a singular act like the pointless killing of a snake, she suggests, is rooted in a culture and what it teaches – 'the voices of [the] accursed human education' that D.H. Lawrence also blames for his own pointless aggression towards a snake.[11] It is not as isolated individuals that we are responsible for the deaths and suffering of the billions of creatures we eat, but as willing participants in collective practices of buying and eating the flesh of animals, in a whole economy, industry and culture that one author has usefully labelled 'carnism'.[12] Misanthropes may prefer to speak of humankind or human forms of life, rather than of the human species, but as we saw in Chapter 1 they essentially endorse Alice Walker's judgement that we are guilty 'as a species'.

ANIMAL SUFFERING AND HUMAN FAILINGS

In place, then, is a catalogue not only of the wrongs done to animals, but of some significant features of this mistreatment. On this basis, we can address the two questions that matter to the misanthrope. First, what is it exactly that makes it a catalogue of *wrongs*? What, in other words, makes so much of our treatment of animals a moral crime? Second, how does reflection on these wrongs serve to confirm the misanthropic verdict on human-kind as being — to recall the Australian policeman's words — lower than any other kind of animal?

The answer to the first question is that our treatment of animals is wrong, a moral crime, because it manifests the vices and other broadly moral failings exposed in Chapter 4. This is part of the answer, too, to the second question, but the misanthrope needs to say something further, to explain in effect why reflection on our treatment of animals adds to and enhances the case against humankind. This is something the misanthrope under-takes in the next chapter. The present task is to elaborate on the answer to the question of what makes the charge list one of wrongs against animals.

Some people may feel that answers to such questions as why it is wrong to keep calves immobile and in total darkness, or to skin a snake alive, or to compel bears to dance are too obvious to require elaboration. The misanthrope has some sympathy with this response, but it's rather too quick. For a start, it is worth recalling that there have been people for whom it's not even obvious *that* it's wrong to do such things. St Thomas Aquinas held that, since animals are 'intended for man's use . . . it is no wrong for man to make use of them, either by killing or in any other way whatever'.[13] Four centuries later, Benedict Spinoza argued that we may 'consult our own advantage and use them [animals] as we please, treating them in the way that best suits us'.[14] And even in 1974, a scientist who was asked 'Don't animals count at all?' could answer 'Why should they?'.[15]

Second, we should distinguish between its being obvious that a practice is wrong and its being obvious why it's wrong. Among philosophers who do take it that animals should be treated con-siderately — most of them, one hopes — there are differences over what it is that makes treatment of them wrong. Kant, for example, thought that we should 'practice kindness towards ani-mals', but that the only genuinely moral reason for this is that otherwise we might become unkind and 'hard' in our dealings with people.[16] By contrast, the favoured approach, these days, is in terms of the alleged rights and moral status of animals. It's wrong to cause pigeons gratuitous harm, states one contemporary philosopher, because 'pigeons . . . have *moral status*' and hence have '*moral rights*'.[17] Maltreatment of animals, then, consists in a failure to recognise or honour their status and rights.

There are several legitimate worries about this approach, some of which will be aired in Chapter 9. But the misanthrope's immediate concern is that it downplays or masks the role of our failings in the understanding of crimes against animals. These wrongs, it seems on this approach, are the result of a kind of philosophical error, a fault of moral reason in failing to extend rights beyond human beings to other creatures. This might indeed be a failing, but it is not, for the misanthrope, the only or the main one that our treatment of animals reflects.

The misanthrope's claim is that, in a sense, it is obvious what is wrong with our usage of animals, for it is evident that it manifests our vices and failings, and this is what is wrong with it.[18] Crudely put, our treatment of animals is bad because we are bad – or, more circumspectly, because the human forms or ways of life in which we are generally willing participants are bad, shot through with vices and failings. No other account of our maltreatment of animals encourages us, as we should be encouraged, to turn the spotlight on ourselves and our ways of life so that these failings are made palpable and prominent in our collective self-perception. This does not mean that we should not be attending to the animals themselves. Indeed, failure of attention to what they are like and to how our actions affect them is itself a moral failing.

What remains is for the misanthrope to indicate to any sceptics there might be how the forms of mistreatment on the charge list do reflect our failings. This means recalling an earlier charge list, from Chapter 4, where these failings were loosely gathered into a number of connected clusters. How are these clusters represented in the wrongs done to animals? Hatred and its relatives are easily recognisable in people's malevolent attitudes towards what they regard as vermin and pests; but also in the once common demonisation of wolves, or in the scapegoating of foxes and badgers for livestock deaths that more efficient husbandry and expenditure on inoculations could prevent. Boorishness, vulgarity and other members of the 'loutishness' cluster are visible in the degrading treatment to which dancing bears, performing dolphins and contestants in 'The World's Ugliest Dog' competition are subjected, in casual everyday acts of aggression towards passing dogs and cats, and in the tossing of toxic rubbish in places where wildlife tries to survive.

Negligence, insensitivity and other failings in the 'mindlessness' cluster are manifested by, for example, irresponsible pet owners who leave their animals hungry or lonely, by boatmen who ignore the effects on whales or fish of their engines and effluence, or by nearly all of us in our inattention to how our way of life impacts on the habitats of birds and other wild animals. Such failings shade into those belonging in the 'bad faith' cluster. These are displayed by, among much else, the betrayal of pets by owners who discard them, the wilful ignorance of racing enthusiasts or anglers in denial about the suffering that their sport involves, and the hypocrisy of people who complain against experimentation on dogs but stay silent when the dogs are substituted by rats.

The vices in the 'vanity' cluster are easily observed in the boasting of shooters, in wearing fur and carrying bags made of reptile skins, in the conceit that a small advantage to human beings warrants the sacrifice of any number of animals, and – a topic for the next chapter – in a collective hubris that regards animals as raw material for the use of humankind. Finally, the effects of the failings in the 'greed' cluster are everywhere evident in our treatment of animals: in the excesses of recreational hunting, the seizing of monkeys from their jungle homes to supply a taste for exotic pets, the murder of rhinos for powdered horn that is imagined to increase virility and so on.

Failings in each of the clusters are, unsurprisingly, on parade in the set of practices responsible for the greatest mass of animal suffering, those that comprise our cultures of food. These failings are manifest in the callousness and brutality of some of the people who debeak, shear or slaughter animals without concern for the pain inflicted. Manifest, too, in the indifference and wilful ignorance of a public content to put out of mind the impact of their supermarket purchases on the lives of the animals they eat. This is made easier for the public by the deceit and disingenuousness, integral to a 'carnist' economy, of an industry that is allowed to describe as 'free range' creatures who never step outside of a factory, to advertise the eating of meat as a necessity, to portray grinning pigs as eager to be converted into bacon, or to present outdated forms of slaughter as divine requirements. It is vanity – a pursuit of status and a display of luxury – as much or more than the demands of a refined palate that condemns geese, veal calves and lobsters to their dreadful lives or deaths. And it is greed – the vice of greed, that is, not simple hunger – that impels people to demand that they can have, at every meal, meat at a cheap price that only animal factories can provide. Not all consumers are like the sweating, red-faced customers struggling to complete the 'challenges' that some restaurants like to lay down – to eat a mountain of steak, chops, pulled pork, sausages, chicken and bacon, for example. But such 'challenges' are not a bad metaphor for what has become an established way of food in the developed world.

CONCLUSION

The misanthrope will want to contrast this culture of food with a better one, a more 'wholesome' one, as Buddhists put it: a way marked by simplicity, transparency, mindfulness and compassion. But that's for a later chapter; the task in the present chapter has been to show the wrongs done to animals and why these are wrongs. Simply put, what is wrong in the treatment of animals is us – the failings and vices of humankind as it has become. There may be other ways of understanding or characterising these wrongs. Perhaps, as utilitarians hold, they reduce the greatest happiness of the greatest number; or perhaps they defy the love that God feels for all creatures and expects us to feel as well; or perhaps they violate the rights of animals.

The misanthrope has no need to argue for or against such views, but simply observes that none of them, as they stand, capture what is of the essence: the manifestation in our treatment of animals of what is worst in the human way of life. There is no need, the misanthrope feels, for elaborate philosophical argument – for constructing a set of moral principles and deducing from them what is right and wrong – in order to see and show why what is done to animals is a moral crime. One philosopher recalls a youthful episode when he and some friends unskilfully slaughtered a terrified and agonised turkey. He explains that their brutality was not due to some philosophical error in moral reason: it was the result neither of a failure to recognise 'some basic equality [of rights] between people and animals', nor of a 'speciesist' refusal to recognise the moral status of animals. Instead, 'we were simply the standard stone-hearted products of a society in which the living animal is merely a transition phase on the way to becoming food'.[19]

This stone-heartedness is precisely the kind of failing that the misanthrope wants to expose, and once exposed there is then no further question as to why it is bad to inflict suffering on a turkey or any other animal for the trivial benefits of a tasty dinner, a day's fun with a rifle or yet another new hair shampoo. 'See' and 'show' are important words in the misanthrope's account. The aim is to show us the wrongs done to animals and the clusters of failings that these reflect. If the misanthrope succeeds in this aim, then it is left to us to see what is wrong with us and what we do.

Well, not quite perhaps . . . and the misanthrope's work is not yet done. For it will modulate and deepen our perception of what is wrong in our treatment of animals to consider what may make it a peculiarly fundamental human failure. It is to this that the misanthrope turns in the following chapter.

NOTES

1 Louis de Bernières, *Red Dog*, London: Vintage, 2002, pp. 105–6.

2 Isaac Bashevis Singer, 'The Letter Writer', in *Collected Stories*, London: Penguin, 2011, pp. 271–2.

3 J. M. Coetzee, *The Lives of Animals*, Princeton: Princeton University Press, 1999, pp. 21, 58, 69.

4 Kundera, *The Unbearable Lightness of Being*, London: Faber & Faber, p. 289.

5 The books include Peter Singer, *Animal Liberation*, London: Bodley Head, 1975; Jim Mason, *An Unnatural Order: The Roots of Our Destruction of Nature*, op. cit.; Charles Patterson, *Eternal Treblinka: Our Treatment of Animals and the Holocaust*, New York: Lantern, 2002; and Hal Herzog, *Some We Love, Some We Hate, Some We Eat: Why Is It So Hard To Think about Animals?* New York: Harper Perennial, 2011.

6 Ruth Harrison, *Animal Machines*, London: Stuart and Watkins, 1964.

7 Brook Ziporyn (tr.), *Zhuangzi: The Essential Writings*, Indianapolis, IN: Hackett, 2009, p. 83.

8 Plutarch, 'The Eating of Flesh', in L. Kalof and A. Fitzgerald (eds.), *The Animals Reader*, Oxford: Berg, 2007, p. 156.

9 Margaret Atwood, 'It's Autumn', in G. Gibson (ed.), *The Bedside Book of Beasts*, London: Bloomsbury, 2009.

10 Alice Walker, 'Everything Is a Human Being', in *Living By The Word: Selected Writings 1973–87*, London: Weidenfeld & Nicolson (Kindle ed.), 2011.

11 D. H. Lawrence, 'The Snake', in *The Complete Poems of D. H. Lawrence*, Ware: Wordsworth Editions, 1994, p. 284.

12 Melanie Joy, *Why We Love Dogs, Eat Pigs, and Wear Cows: An Introduction to Carnism*, San Francisco, CA: Red Wheel Weiser, 2010.

13 Quoted in T. Regan and P. Singer (eds.), *Animal Rights and Human Obligations*, Englewood Cliffs, NJ: Prentice Hall, 1989, p. 8.

14 Quoted in Mary Midgley, *Animals and Why They Matter*, London: Penguin, 1983, p. 10.

15 Ibid.

16 Immanuel Kant, *Lectures on Ethics*, New York: Harper & Row, 1963, p. 240.

17 David DeGrazia, *Animal Rights: A Very Short Introduction*, Oxford: Oxford University Press, 2002, pp. 37–8.

18 The misanthrope in effect agrees with so-called 'virtue ethicists' that in asking whether practices are wrong, we should ask whether they manifest virtues or vices. For a clear account, see Rosalind Hursthouse, 'Applying Virtue Ethics to Our Treatment of Other Animals', in J. Weichman (ed.), *The Practice of Virtue: Classic and Contemporary Readings in Virtue Ethics*, Indianapolis, IN: Hackett, 2006, pp. 136–55.

19 Tzachi Zamir, *Ethics and the Beast: A Speciesist Argument for Animal Liberation*, Princeton, NJ: Princeton University Press, 2007, p. 136.

7

'A FUNDAMENTAL DEBACLE'

Why is it that misanthropes want to talk about our treatment of animals at all – about 'brutality to "brutes"' as well as 'inhumanity to humans'? A good enough reason is to show that the scale of humankind's failings is much greater than one would otherwise estimate. Optimistic accounts of humanity's moral progress frequently fail, after all, to mention the plight of animals.[1] But, for misanthropes, it is not only the quantity, but the quality of the wrongs we do that is affected by the way we use animals. Our failings and vices, as manifested in treatment of animals, are in certain respects distinctive. To ignore them is to marginalise or remain blind to dimensions of practices and attitudes that deserve to figure in any broadly moral appraisal of humankind.

AGRICULTURE, HUBRIS, TECHNOLOGY

To explore these dimensions, a good place to start is Milan Kundera's remark on our attitudes to animals as constituting 'a fundamental debacle' (p. 79 above). He gives two reasons for this judgement. One, to which I return in the next section, is that these are attitudes to creatures 'at our mercy'. The other, to which I now turn, is that all our other moral debacles 'follow from' that of our attitudes to animals.

Kundera's point is not the one illustrated in William Hogarth's famous series of prints, 'The Four Stages of Cruelty', in which the criminal career of a very nasty young man is depicted as beginning with his casual cruelty to animals. Kundera's claim is not one about developmental psychology. It's best understood by relating it to a view that has gained currency in recent years, although it can be traced back at least to Rousseau. The view is encapsulated in the title of an influential 1989 article by Jared Diamond, 'The Worst Mistake in the History of the Human Race'.[2] The mistake was agriculture, including husbandry and the domestication of animals. Diamond and his followers argue that this development was the precondition of most of the ills of history. Wars of conquest, slavery, the subjection of women, despotism and much else were made possible and encouraged by the demands of an agricultural economy.

Misanthropes are less interested in the social and political consequences of agriculture in general than in a moral and 'spiritual bankruptcy' that, as they see it, grows alongside the spread of animal farming.[3] Their attention is on failings and vices that, while they may not have originated with farming, were facilitated, given scope and opportunity, and became entrenched in agricultural societies. This implies a contrast with hunter-gatherer communities. The misanthrope is far from wanting to romanticise such communities, and is fully aware of the cruel treatment of animals – cooking turtles alive, for example – sometimes permitted by their traditions.[4] But found in these traditions, too, is a respect paid to various animals – especially those that to be successfully hunted had to be understood, like bears, wolves and deer – which is not afforded to the squealing pigs and frightened calves that farmers control, fatten up and slaughter. 'All hunter-gatherers', it's been said, 'had rules about the treatment of animals . . . designed to show and perpetuate goodwill'.[5] These are rules, of course, with which livestock farmers are able dispense.

The respect afforded to many animals is reflected in the religions of hunter-gatherer peoples. Typical of the religions studied by anthropologists are animal spirits, veneration of totemic animals, belief in the transformation of human beings into animals and vice versa and confidence in the shaman's capacity to communicate and negotiate with animals.[6] The contrast with the religions that came to predominate among agricultural peoples in the Middle East and the West is striking. These are religions in which human beings are said to be made in the image of God, who is himself invested with uniquely human attributes, and whose creation of the world is held to have been for the sake of humankind. Further east, even Buddhism, a dispensation more considerate towards animals than the great monotheistic religions, regards rebirth as an animal as the 'woeful' result of karma, worse even than rebirth as a 'hungry ghost'.

What is indicated here is that domestication and husbandry inspire a kind of collective hubris on the part of human beings. This is not the pride of farmers in their efficient management or the quality of the beef they sell, but a hubris spread through human societies that, in Martin Heidegger's words, 'exalts [humankind] to the posture of lord of the earth'.[7] It is a hubris utterly inimical, of course, to the respect, veneration even, that was granted to at least some animals by pre-agricultural peoples. Nor were the consequences of collective hubris confined to farm animals. For example, animals that in any way threatened livestock or crops – wolves, foxes, crows, rats – became vermin or pests to be exterminated and despised for their challenge to human ambitions. Nor, indeed, were the consequences confined to animals. Traditional communities, deemed backward or even sub-human, who occupied lands required for agricultural expansion, grazing or irrigation themselves became perceived as an obstacle and challenge to economic progress. They needed to be removed, enslaved or massacred. Nature itself also became an obstacle and challenge, hence something that had to be subdued, transformed and remoulded to fit in with the imperatives of farming. Rivers need to be diverted, forests cut down, mountains blown up.

Advances in agricultural technology – in what Heidegger called the 'motorised food industry' – confirmed and further intensified this collective hubris. Everything becomes 'equipment', 'standing reserve', so much material 'on tap' for an industry whose capacity for controlling and ordering nature, animals and people knows no limits.[8] Crushed together in batteries before being turned into a pinkish slush that machines then form into sausages, burgers or 'nuggets', chickens and other creatures lose their status as animals, becoming instead the raw material from which to manufacture products. Instead of the nature of an animal being anything to respect or admire, it becomes something to alter, through drugs or genetic engineering, if the manufacturing process is thereby speeded up or made cheaper to run. The same readiness to subject animals to mechanical, chemical or genetic interventions soon spreads from the factory farm to the research laboratory and the specialist pet breeding industry. And it spreads beyond the use of animals to sophisticated means for exploiting nature and murdering people.

By the term 'technology' Heidegger understood not the physical processes of production, but a certain 'way of revealing' the world that these processes manifest – a way that is especially dangerous because of its power to 'drive out every other way of revealing'.[9] It is the way that reveals everything as 'equipment' or 'standing reserve', to be used and drawn upon to further human ambitions. It is, in effect, a form of the vice or failing of mindlessness, discussed in Chapter 4 – the absence, as it was put, of clear, open and responsive attention to the world and to the needs and goods of creatures. Zhuangzi was already acquainted with this when he observed the training, branding, corralling and confinement of horses without regard for the 'true inborn nature of horses'.[10] Whereas the traditional hunter or farmer had to know something about the nature and needs of the animals on whom the survival of his family depended, the modern industrial farmer requires to know only what is relevant to maximising the amount of pork, chicken stuff or beef that he can produce. What it is like to be a pig, what is good for a turkey – these are topics he or she can safely ignore.

Mindlessness, of course, is not confined to farming. To regard foxes, rats or crows simply as vermin or pests is more of the same. Even pets, despite – or because of – their owners' love for them, are often appreciated not for the animals they are, but as the make-believe creatures the owners would like them to be, ones without, for example, sexual desires. As J.R. Ackerley put it in the classic biography of his German shepherd, Tulip, too many pets are 'stupidly loved, stupidly hated, acquired without thought, reared without understanding'.[11] Mindlessness, we know, is not restricted to the realm of animals. The instrumental attitude so evident in the case of animals easily extends to forests and mountains, and to the men and women that other people enslave and perceive as materials or tools.

This discussion began with Kundera's claim that our attitude to animals constitutes a fundamental debacle because other debacles follow from it. If this means that collective hubris and mindlessness originated with husbandry and domestication, and that our other broadly moral failings all developed from these, then of course the claim is much too strong. But it is not at all implausible to hold that hubris and the failure to attend to beings for what they are were facilitated, and provided with an extensive domain for their exercise, by the subjection of animals to human power and purpose in agricultural economies.

Nor is it at all far-fetched to suppose that other vices and failings – greed, indifference, callousness and others – are, if not derived from those two, then fed, encouraged and given scope and direction by them. As we saw in Chapter 4, the vices are related to one another in what Buddhists call a circular chain of 'dependent origination', or 'conditioned arising'. Each is related to every other, and they serve to reinforce one another. But it is more helpful to start with some links rather than others, for they enable a more perspicuous, explanatorily satisfying vision of how the chain operates, how the links are connected to one another. The collective hubris and mindlessness that became entrenched through the usage of animals in farming are two very closely connected links that we do well to begin with in attempting to achieve such a vision. In this respect, it is not wayward to describe them, and the moral debacle they represent, as 'fundamental'.

A 'TRUE MORAL TEST'

There is a second respect, according to Kundera, in which our attitude to animals is fundamentally wrong. It fails to pass 'mankind's true moral test', which is to demonstrate an attitude of compassion, care and concern for those who are at our mercy. A comparable remark is often, but probably mistakenly, attributed to Mahatma Gandhi. 'One can measure the greatness of a nation and its moral progress by the way it treats its animals', precisely because they are 'helpless and weak' in comparison to humankind.[12] It's not being denied that there are other classes of beings – most obviously, children – who are also at people's mercy. But if these remarks are well-taken, then there is a quality to our ill-treatment of animals, children and other helpless and dependent beings that singles it out from the general wrongs for which people are responsible.

Should we, however, accept these claims about the true measure or test of an authentically moral attitude? The misanthrope's strategy is not to conjure up some set of principles that give pride of place to concern for the helpless and dependent, but to appeal to people's ordinary moral intuitions, their own moral self-image, and to reflect on the implications of these. Doing so will indeed reveal that our treatment of animals is impossible to reconcile with the place that people like to imagine goodness has in human life.

That concern for those at our mercy, for the dependent and weak, is a central plank of morality is not the idiosyncratic opinion of Kundera, Gandhi or any other individual person. The teachings of Jesus, the Buddha, Mahavira, St Francis of Assisi and countless other moral and religious educators emphasise the centrality of this concern.[13] In these teachings, concern is not, of course, confined to animals: children, women, the sick and the poor are also mentioned as especially deserving of moral concern. This special concern is not proclaimed only by teachers like those just mentioned: it is something nearly all of us endorse. But it is also something that most of us fail, for much of the time, to put into practice. Sufficient proof of this is the catalogue of crimes against animals described in the previous chapter. But one could easily add further catalogues – of the oppressive subjection of women in many societies, of the neglected condition in some countries of the lowest and poorest castes, and of the cruel fates of indigenous peoples at the hands of militarily superior invaders.

So, there is much hypocrisy and lip-service in proclamations of the priority of moral concern for the dependent and helpless. But here, as elsewhere, hypocrisy is, as La Rochefoucauld observed, an implicit acknowledgement of virtue by people who are far from regularly practising it. Why pay so much lip-service to something unless it is recognised, deep down, as something one should be honouring? Practice and proclamation may be at odds, but why continue to proclaim the importance of concern for those who are at our mercy unless, in our honest moments, we recognise that failure to practise it is also a fundamental failing?

There is a good reason for being loath to reject or question the moral centrality of concern for the helpless. For, to do so would be to admit something we are even more reluctant to confront – the fragility of goodness. This phrase occurred in Chapter 4 when I argued for the entrenched nature of vices and failings in human life. What was meant was that the virtues flourish only under certain conditions. Remove those conditions and the virtues display their fragility: people once more manifest their worst failings. One of those conditions, as Thomas Hobbes saw so clearly, was the existence of sanctions against causing harm and doing wrong. He saw the application of these sanctions as the preserve of the sovereign, the state. But equally important is the loose system of sanctions that exists among people who are connected to each other in 'a chain of reciprocity'. 'I scratch your back, you scratch mine', 'An eye for an eye, a tooth for a tooth' – such nuggets of folk wisdom indicate that when we benefit or harm our fellows, we can expect them to reciprocate. This provides a rational self-interested motive for, in the main, treating them well and not harming them.

A crucial implication of this point is that, where reciprocity is absent – where, say, there is little chance of anyone I hurt hurting me back – so is a main motive for treating others well. And this, of course, is precisely the situation that obtains with our relationship to animals. 'Chain of reciprocity' is the expression used by the Australian environmental philosopher, Val Plumwood, when explaining how we come to treat animals so inhumanely. 'Animals can be our food, but we can never [or hardly ever] be their food', and more generally, they cannot subject us to the indignities, cruelties and other harms that we, with impunity, can visit on them.[14] A partial exception, and only to a degree, may be found in the complex relationships some people have with their pets. Unless a dog is treated well, he fails to show the affection and loyalty that his owner wants and hopes for from the dog. He may 'take it out' on his owner. But this is a small dent in the general truth that, in our non-reciprocal relationship with animals, goodness becomes very fragile, for the conditions under which there is a self-interested premium on treating creatures well do not obtain.

To give up the claim – hypocritical though it may often be – that compassion for the dependent and helpless is central to morality is therefore openly to concede the fragility of goodness, to admit that morality loses its hold when extended beyond the domain of reciprocity and mutual advantage. And this is a concession that few people can be happy to make, for it belongs to the self-image of morality that it is practised 'for its own sake'. That it is a central component in this self-image demonstrates the truth in Kundera's proposal that how we treat those at our mercy is our 'true moral test'. It is not just Kundera, but nearly all of us, who like to believe that goodness and virtue are sufficiently robust and entrenched to be practised irrespective of any advantage to ourselves. The test of this belief is how we treat those who cannot reciprocate, a test that is so signally failed in the case of animals. It is not over-dramatic to describe as a debacle the failure to pass a test so fundamental to the self-understanding of ourselves as moral beings.

It is worth emphasising that the failure, the debacle, is not only – or even primarily – that of individual persons. To be sure, there are plenty of individual men and women whose concern and compassion is strictly confined to those creatures they encounter in a chain of reciprocity. But the larger failure belongs to something more amorphous, more 'collective' – the institution of morality, a way of life, modern society, humankind. As argued in earlier chapters, the failure of you and me to extend concern to, say, the helpless victims of the 'motorised food industry', is the failure of people who participate in, fall in with, practices integral to the kind of society and culture that we find ourselves members of. Relevant to this and other considerations about our fundamental debacle is a controversial analogy to which I now turn.

'AN ETERNAL TREBLINKA'?

To be a distinctive, fundamental form of wrong, a practice does not have to be unique or *sui generis*, for it can still have a quality that distinguishes it from the ordinary run of wrong-doing. One way in which misanthropes have tried to show that our treatment of animals is a fundamental moral failure is by comparing it with the holocaust, an event that nearly all commentators regard as an especially evil episode in human history.

When, in a lecture of 1949, Heidegger compared the 'motorised food industry' with the 'manufacture of corpses and the gas chambers',[15] his remark – omitted from the published version of the lecture – caused anger, particularly among Jewish survivors of the camps. Similar comparisons have continued to invite hostile reactions, including Isaac Bashevis Singer's reference, endorsed by J.M. Coetzee, to the condition of the billions of victims of factory farming as 'an eternal Treblinka'. A 2003 campaign launched by the animal welfare organisation PETA, called 'Holocaust on your plate', was banned in Germany. Such comparisons, it is argued, ignore the *sui generis* character of the holocaust, and only serve to 'trivialise' it and render it 'banal'.[16]

It helps to cool the temperature of the controversy to emphasise that Heidegger, Singer and others were only drawing an analogy, without any intention to deny obvious differences between the real Treblinka – the Polish extermination camp – and factory farms or animal research laboratories. The most obvious of these, of course, is that the victims at Treblinka and Auschwitz were men, women and children, not animals. Still, unless one thinks that confining animals in terrible conditions and then killing them does not matter at all, the moral significance of this difference is not clear. Most people agree that human beings count for more than animals, and any realistic account of morality must record this. Although some people care more about the fate of a pet than that of any person, it is part of our prevailing moral perspective that, in general, people 'come first'. Gandhi, for example, endorses this perspective when remarking that it is not right to 'to be kind to [animal] life in preference to human life'.[17] But it's perfectly possible to accept this without thinking that analogies between animal and human suffering in any way trivialise the latter. Only someone who is unwilling to distinguish between harming animals and damaging inanimate objects – between 'chopping up a live dog and a live lettuce', as Lorenz put it[18] – could think that.

Other reasons for dismissing the analogy are uncompelling. It's alleged, for example, that the holocaust manifested hatred towards Jewish people, whereas no hatred is felt towards the animals we eat. This may be true, but it needs qualifying. To begin with, it is unclear that all or even most of the people involved in facilitating and administering the holocaust hated Jews. And while carnivores may not hate cows or chickens, we have seen that hatred is certainly a factor in many massacres of certain kinds of animal – wolves, grey squirrels, rattlesnakes, those classified as vermin and pests. The analogy between Jews and hated animals is one that the Nazis themselves were quick to recognise and exploit, for example in posters and films that portrayed Jews with the features and habits of rodents.

Again, it's been said that while there were ideological and doctrinal motives for the holocaust, 'human beings have no ideological or theological conflict with animals'.[19] But while animals may not challenge our convictions, it is certainly not true that ideology and religion play no role in our crimes against animals. 'Carnism' is not just a culinary preference, but a culture of eating maintained and defended by beliefs about the standing and role of animals in relation to human ends. The collective hubris discussed earlier in this chapter – one reflected in and reinforced by theological doctrines that elevate humankind above the rest of creation – is among the most pernicious and entrenched attitudes responsible for our treatment of animals. It is an attitude, moreover, that easily extends to those people deemed, to borrow from Nazi rhetoric, to be 'sub-human' and 'parasites' on a culture they have invaded. Worth mentioning, too, is a form of Social Darwinism that German – and not just German – writers at the turn of the twentieth century deployed in defence both of eating animals and subjugating or even exterminating races held to be inferior. Creatures, animal or human, who have failed in the evolutionary struggle for the survival of the fittest deserve no pity or consideration.

Differences between human and animal Treblinkas of course exist, but it is legitimate and instructive to draw certain parallels between the vices that are manifested in both cases. To begin with, we find that familiar combination of the callousness and cruelty of the people most directly involved in the infliction of suffering and the wilful ignorance or indifference of large numbers of other people. Professors who drove dogs or monkeys insane with pain or sensory deprivation in the name of scientific research deserve comparison with those who froze Jewish prisoners in the name of the same.[20] The millions of people who ignore or refuse to acknowledge what happens in battery farms are comparable with the millions of Germans who did the same with respect to the death camps.[21]

Evident in both cases, too, are the failings or vices that enable people to treat intelligent beings as resources, as 'standing reserve' on tap for their use. (This was Heidegger's main point in comparing the death camps with industrial farms.) The bodies of some Jewish victims – their hair, skin and teeth – were literally used by wartime German manufacturers as raw material. But all the victims were anyway reduced to the status of a resource, as slaves to be used up and dispensed with when they became too weak to work. This replicates a standard perception of many kinds of animal as having no purpose but to serve and die in obedience to the imperatives of production.

Finally, in both cases, we witness not simply callousness towards the helpless, but a brutality – and scorn, contempt and Schadenfreude – inspired by this very helplessness. Individual concentration camp officials would submit prisoners to gratuitous cruelty or force them to perform obscene and humiliating acts. We know how something similar occurs in abattoirs, zoos, circuses and research laboratories. Here we find the culmination of the atrophy of regard and respect for animals that accompanied the development of husbandry and domestication. And, if the suggestion made earlier in this chapter is right, then the contempt for their helpless victims of some death camp guards was also a culmination and extension of the same long and unhappy development. More generally, both the treatment of Jews in the Third Reich and that of animals just about everywhere demonstrates what can happen to beings who do not belong in a chain of reciprocity. Once it became clear that Europe's Jews could do little to resist their oppressors – that there was little to lose and perhaps something to gain by joining in with the oppression – there was no shortage of people willing to betray their Jewish neighbours, denounce their Jewish colleagues, steal their belongings and take their jobs.

It does nothing to trivialise the holocaust and render it banal to attend to human failings and vices that are as manifest in the treatment of animals as they were in the enslavement and extermination of European Jewry. Indeed, if there is truth in the idea that these failings were magnified, given scope and, as it were, honed through the conversion of animals into livestock – into a resource – then the analogy helps to explain how an event like the holocaust could ever have become a possibility.

In Chapter 6, the misanthrope drew up a charge list of moral crimes that human beings commit against animals; indicated some important aspects of them, including their scale and the casualness with which they are performed; and argued that these are moral crimes precisely because they issue from our vices and other failings. In the present chapter, the misanthrope's purpose has been to reflect on what makes our treatment of animals a distinctive kind of wrong, a 'fundamental debacle' in our moral history – hence something that needs attending to in addition to inhumanity to humans. It does not matter much, perhaps, whether at the end of the day one applies terms like 'fundamental' and 'distinctive' to the wrongs done against animals. What is important is to appreciate why it should seem compelling to some people to reach for such terms – to appreciate, that is, how the collective hubris and mindlessness, and the cruelty or indifference towards creatures at our mercy, on which the misanthrope focused, invites an uncompromisingly harsh judgement on humankind.

It helps, in the misanthrope's view, to bring these aspects, these failings, into relief if we reflect on the metaphor of animals passing through an eternal Treblinka. Again, what finally matters is not whether one accepts or rejects the metaphor, but to understand what makes it sound, to many ears, an apt one, and hence to recognise a deep affinity between the vices and failings responsible for the holocaust and those at work in our treatment of animals. There is nothing morally questionable in pursuing the analogy in attempting to show that there is something distinctive and fundamental about the moral crimes committed against animals. No one thinks that the holocaust was just 'more of the same', just one more run-of-the-mill chapter in the history of evil. But it doesn't follow from this that its evil was unique or incomparable.

This completes the misanthrope's case for a negative moral assessment of humankind. Reflection on our treatment of animals, like the comparison between humankind and animals, has confirmed this assessment. It would be disappointing, though, if the misanthrope could provide no guidance on how, in our lives, we might respond to this verdict. It is to the question of an appropriate response that we now turn.

NOTES

1 Animals are not mentioned, for example, by either of the contributors who answer 'Yes' to the question posed by the debate in *Do Humankind's Best Days Lie Ahead?: Munk Debate 2015*, London: OneWorld, 2016.

2 *Discover*, May 1987, pp. 64–6.

3 Jim Mason, *An Unnatural Order: The Roots of Our Destruction of Nature*, New York: Lantern, 1993, p. 161.

4 For examples, see Steven Pinker, *The Better Angels of Our Nature*, London: Penguin, 2011, pp. 551ff.

5 Hugh Brody, *The Other Side of Eden: Hunter-Gatherers, Farmers and the Shaping of the World*, London: Faber & Faber, 2001, p. 254.

6 See Steven Mithen, 'The Hunter-Gatherer Prehistory of Human-Animal Interactions', *Anthrozoos*, 12, 1999, pp. 195–204.

7 Martin Heidegger, *The Question Concerning Technology and Other Essays*, New York: Harper & Row, 1977, p. 27.

8 Ibid., pp. 15ff.

9 Ibid., p. 27.

10 Brook Ziporyn (tr.), *Zhuangzi: The Essential Writings*, Indianapolis, IN: Hackett, 2009, p. 60.

11 J. R. Ackerley, *My Dog Tulip*, New York: New York Review of Books, 1999, p. 187.

12 See Philip Johnson, http://animalsmattertogod.com/2013/09/13/mahatma-gandhi-hoax-quote-greatness-of-a-nation-and-its-moral-progress-can-be-judged-by-the-way-that-its-animals-are-treated/

13 See Matthieu Ricard, *A Plea for the Animals: The Moral, Philosophical and Evolutionary Imperative to Treat All Beings with Compassion*, Boston: Shambala, 2016, Chapter 1.

14 Quoted in Jeffrey Masson, *Beasts: What Animals Can Teach Us about the Origins of Good and Evil*, New York: Bloomsbury, 2014, pp. 7–8.

15 Quoted and discussed in Rüdiger Safranski, *Martin Heidegger: Between Good and Evil*, Cambridge, MA: Harvard University Press, 1999, p. 414.

16 For these and other reactions, see Charles Patterson, *Eternal Treblinka*, New York: Lantern, op. cit.

17 Gandhi, *The Collected Works of Mahatma Gandhi*, Ahmedabad: Navajivan, Vol. 91, p. 61.

18 Konrad Lorenz, *On Aggression*, London: Routledge, 2004, p. 219.

19 Roberta Kalechovsky, quoted in 'Animal Rights and the Holocaust', *Wikipedia*, p. 3.

20 See Bernard E. Rollin, 'Antivivisectionism, Animal Experimentation, and Nazism', *Anthrozoös*, VI, 1992, pp. 93–6.

21 For the classic account of these 'bystanders', see Daniel J. Goldhagen, *Hitler's Willing Executioners: Ordinary Germans and the Holocaust*, London: Abacus, 1997.

8

RESPONDING TO
MISANTHROPY

A comparison of human life with the lives of animals combines with attention to our treatment of animals to confirm a misanthropic verdict on humankind. How, if at all, should people respond to this verdict? Many of history's famous misanthropes – Schopenhauer, Leopardi and Freud, for example – state that their writings are motivated by a desire not simply to inform people that, as Leopardi puts it, 'the world is the enemy of the good',[1] but to help them to improve how they live or at any rate to cope better with their condition. By holding up a mirror to the moral ugliness of humankind, some people at least may be inspired to resist or distance themselves from it. The aim is not that people should simply look in the mirror and say 'Oh, dear!'.

Someone may, of course, respond to the image in the mirror by denying its accuracy, by rejecting the misanthropic verdict, that is. Since this is tantamount to rejecting the arguments and conclusions of the preceding chapters, I can only ask readers tempted by this response to look again at these chapters. Among those who accept the verdict, responses vary from attempts to soften its force to radical programmes for the elimination of human failings to quieter accommodations to the truth of misanthropy. In this chapter, I consider some of these responses before, in Chapter 9, turning to ways in which relating to animals belongs in an authentic accommodation to misanthropy.

OPTIMISM

It is easy to understand why people seek to resist or deflect the misanthropic verdict. It is a dark, uncomfortable verdict, even if some misanthropes – Leopardi and Emil Cioran, for instance – seem to thrive on their passionate denunciations of human life. Less easy to understand are some of the arguments used to refute misanthropy. It's been suggested, for example, that misanthropy is 'finally impossible', a 'fundamental contradiction', since the misanthrope has 'contempt' for everyone, including himself, and therefore 'stands self-condemned'.[2] It's not made clear, however, what is impossible about self-condemnation. Self-loathing, sadly, seems to be far from self-contradictory. Moreover, the objection assumes that the target of misanthropy is each and every human being. But it is something more 'collective' or 'abstract' – humankind, human forms of life – that, as we've often noted, is the primary target. There is no tension between a severe verdict on humankind and respect or fondness for particular people including, with any luck, one's self. This was Jonathan Swift's point when declaring, in a letter to Alexander Pope, that he could 'heartily love John, Peter, Thomas and so forth' while 'hat[ing] and detest[ing] that animal called man'.[3]

The most common strategy for softening the force of the misanthropic verdict is optimism. According to the optimist, the verdict may once have been well deserved, but humankind has progressed, and if the verdict is not already out of date, it surely will be soon. It is, of course, easy to imagine utopian scenarios – like the ones sometimes portrayed on the covers of Jehovah Witnesses' magazines – in which all beings live in virtue, happiness and peace. But even if such scenarios were ever to be realised, this would only threaten the verdict if their realisation was the work of human beings and if, in the scenarios, it is still human beings – living a recognisably human form of life – that are present. It does nothing to disturb the verdict if utopia is the result, not of human good will and effort, but of divine grace or Schopenhauer's salvific 'gleam of silver' that 'suddenly appears' and destroys the roots of suffering and evil.[4] Nor is it threatened if the occupants of the utopian scenarios are no longer human beings, but angelic, saintly creatures who have transcended their humanity, who is effect belong to another species.[5] One reason it is right to regard Buddhism as a misanthropic dispensation is that, while a person may strive for enlightenment and emancipation, success consists in liberation from the human condition. An enlightened person, a buddha, may remain in the world for a time, but is no longer 'of the world', released as he or she is, not only from the cycle of rebirth, but from the chain of desires, perceptions, ignorance and ambitions that constitute the human lot.

So, the question for the optimist concerns the prospects for people still living recognisably human lives to eliminate or reduce failings and vices. These prospects need to be good in order to invalidate the misanthrope's judgement on humankind. The optimist is someone who thinks that the prospects are not only good but that, in modern times, substantial progress has already been made towards their realisation.

The best-known work of optimism in recent years is Steven Pinker's 2011 book, *The Better Angels of Our Nature*. We should, he argues, 'marvel at the moral advances' of the last few decades, and expect these advances, like those in technology, medicine and science, to continue.[6] But I am not the only reader to come away from this book impressed less by its up-beat account of a century of progress than by its massively documented demonstration of 'how much suffering has been inflicted', over millennia, 'by the naked ape upon its own kind' and other species. When he is exposing 'our drives for dominance and revenge', our treatment of many people as 'vermin', our 'self-serving biases', or our liability to 'collective delusion', Pinker sounds to be making the case for, not against, misanthropy.[7] Progress there may have been in some areas in recent times, but the base – as Pinker's own historical chapters prove – was a very low one. Progress indeed needs to have been on a scale to marvel at if it is to be cited in support of overturning the misanthropic verdict.

The subtitle of Pinker's book is 'A History of Violence and Humanity', and it is the decline of violence and of the vices that most directly inspire it – the urge to dominate people, for example – on which his optimistic conclusion is based. Very little is said to suggest that other failings and vices – those, for example, of vanity, mean mindedness, vulgarity, envy, overambition and bad faith – are being extinguished or even moderated. If Pinker's focus on our vices is circumscribed, so is his perception of our virtues. What confirms for him the moral progress that we are making is a growing and impeccably liberal attachment to the 'cardinal virtues' of 'fairness and autonomy'.[8] He is, in effect, a prime representative of that thin conception of morality that prevails in modern, especially American, moral philosophy that I have alluded to at several points – the idea that morality is only or essentially a matter of respect for rights and justice. It is a conception on which there is little, if any, mention of virtues that figure in traditional visions of the good life. So, it is no surprise that Pinker writes little or nothing to suggest that, over the last few decades, such virtues as humility, self-honesty and compassion are prospering. Indeed, it is not surprising to find him recording his worry that compassion and its relatives could 'subvert' the truly 'fundamental principle' of fairness.[9]

Finally, Pinker's perception of progress in the form of declining violence is called into question by our treatment of animals. Today's naked ape may inflict less suffering on its own kind than earlier, but it continues to inflict a great deal on other species. Pinker, to his credit, does not, as so many optimists do, ignore our treatment of animals; over twenty pages are devoted to 'Animal Rights and the Decline of Cruelty to Animals'. But his discussion is, to begin with, remarkably parochial, focused almost entirely on the United States where, allegedly, vegetarianism is increasing, recreational hunting declining and the number of animal experiments reducing. Attention to other parts of the world, however, would show that the number of animals killed to be eaten continues to grow massively (especially in China and India), that shooting birds and fishing for the fun of it is a mushrooming industry (in the United Kingdom and eastern Europe, for example) and experimentation is on the rise (in Russia, the UK and Spain, for instance). Pinker himself admits that 'meat hunger and the social pleasures that go with the consumption of meat' are a serious obstacle to improving the lot of billions of animals.[10]

Second, he makes no mention of the growing numbers of creatures, in the United States included, that suffer as the result of some distinctively modern fashions. Nothing is said, for example, about the flourishing trade in wild animals – or bits of them, like their horns – that is responsible for the painful deaths or kidnapping of tens of thousands of monkeys, elephants, snakes or crocodiles each year. Nor is there any reference to the cruelties of the ever-expanding pet industry – to discarded puppies, say, or to the culling of redundant cats, or to purebred bitches forced to have one litter after another until, exhausted, they are put down. Bear-baiting may have gone, but no one who reads the literature on which I drew in Chapter 6, on our treatment of animals, could share Pinker's sunny optimism that 'it is certain that the lives of animals will continue to improve'.[11]

Pinker's optimism is unlikely to convert people sympathetic to misanthropy. Indeed, they will see in his attachment to a conception of morality that encourages a rosy perception of recent moral progress a diversion from robust attention to the failings and vices that the misanthrope identifies. They will remind themselves, too, how several of these vices – hypocrisy, vanity, bad faith – serve to protect people from honest appreciation of the extent of these failings. And they will recall, too, a number of general factors – the hedonism of our age, the harsh imperatives of modern economies, the sheer 'busy-ness' of life and much else – that are not only very much still with us but provide the context in which many of our failings and vices are enabled to flourish and become entrenched.

RADICALISM

'Low-mindedness, coldness, egoism, avarice, falsity and treachery', declared Leopardi, are not going to fade away as part of an optimistically imagined movement of 'moral progress', and we should therefore 'accept all the consequences of a philosophy that is grievous, but true'. The poet's own response to his embrace of this philosophy is that one should 'live and be great and unhappy'.[12] It's not entirely clear what he intended by these words, but similarly dramatic remarks by other misanthropes sometimes herald a determination to find radical solutions to the moral plight of humankind.

By exhorting us to live with the 'grievous' truth of misanthropy, Leopardi is excluding, of course, the most radical solution of all – the extinction of our species. The nineteenth-century pessimist philosopher, Eduard von Hartmann, hoped that his demonstration of the impossibility of living well and happily would, in the fullness of time, encourage the collective suicide of humanity.[13] Some contemporary pessimists and misanthropists embrace, as we've seen, an 'anti-natalist' position that, if universally endorsed, would entail the end of homo sapiens. We have already encountered writers who, while not explicitly calling for extermination, seem to find it a welcome prospect – Ian McHarg, for example, with his description of humankind as a 'planetary disease'. Many others have been at least equivocal in their attitude to the possible destruction of the human race, including Ludwig Wittgenstein who, shortly after Hiroshima and Nagasaki, wonders whether the atomic bomb, since it 'offers a prospect of the end, the destruction, of an evil – our disgusting soapy water science', is something to welcome.[14]

Given the unlikelihood of the demise of our species in the foreseeable future, whether by its own hand or in some other manner, some misanthropists have instead proposed radical strategies for so transforming human existence that the misanthropic verdict would no longer be deserved. Some of these strategies seek to destroy the conditions that, as their champions see it, are largely responsible for many of our current failings and vices. Over-population, for example, is often blamed for evils ranging from wars and grinding poverty to the destruction of environments, including animal habitats. As a result, we hear proposals for radical population reduction, to as little as one-tenth of its present size. Others attribute these and further ills – exploitation, injustice, 'carnism' – to greed, disparities in wealth and the desire of people to enjoy affluent lifestyles. Hence, we are told that 'we must achieve the character and acquire the skills to live much poorer than we do'.[15]

But these proposals are barely less fanciful than ones for universal suicide. If the human population, or the affluence of a large number of people, were to be radically reduced, this would be the outcome of unforeseen events, not of planning and policy. To be sure, there may be people who envisage a more direct strategy than the removal of conditions – like over-population and affluence – deemed responsible for our failings. They may dream – like born-again Red Guards – of a moral revolution, of muscular moral engineering that will reconstruct human society, human nature even, thereby producing a race of people liberated from the vices of their ancestors. The dream may be accompanied by religious zeal, reminiscent of the moral and political ambitions of seventeenth-century Puritan governments or the theocratic Ayatollahs of more recent times. But this is fanciful, too, and the precedents cited for moral engineering on such a scale, like Mao's Cultural Revolution, provide good enough evidence for the hopelessness of an enforced reconstruction of our moral condition.

It is not only the fancifulness of these radical strategies that disqualify them from serious consideration by someone wondering how to respond to the truth of misanthropy. Even if they were less improbable, it is hard to see their relevance to how you or I should respond. For it won't be through anything that you and I do or think that the human population will shrink or that people will agree to 'live much poorer' than they do. What you and I should attend to are not hypothetical scenarios whose realisation we are anyway unable to influence, but how, here and now, we might adjust our lives and attitudes in the light of the misanthropic verdict.

These points apply to proposals regarding our relationship with animals in particular. Here, too, we encounter in the literature radical ambitions to eliminate meat-eating, abolish animal experimentation, outlaw all recreational hunting and so forth. Ironically, though, some of the authors who envisage these outcomes also do a good job in showing why they smack of fantasy. Melanie Joy, for example, holds that the 'carnism' that underlies present practices of eating meat is 'a house of cards', and that its 'power' will soon disappear.[16] But this is a peculiarly optimistic conclusion for a book that skilfully describes both the powerful forces, economic and ideological, that help to encourage these practices and the many strong 'defences' that have been erected around 'carnism'. If 'carnism' is a house of cards, it is one that is riveted together and heavily fortified.

None of this is to suggest that the work of Joy and other activists is worthless. These brave people save lives, prevent the bringing into the world of creatures whose lives would be wretched, reduce the suffering of the ones who have been born – and they inspire others to do the same. But it's possible to admire their work without pretending that it could bring about anything approaching a universal change in our practices and attitudes to animals. It is possible, that is, to admire it without entertaining the prospect of a social revolution in human beings' relationship to animals that could contribute to the refutation of misanthropy.

QUIETISM

Wise misanthropes are under no illusions. It is unlikely that the world and human beings are going to change dramatically for the good, and it is anyway hard to see how you or I could contribute to such a change even if, in some manner, it came about. The modest aim of these misanthropes is to make a personal accommodation, to make the best of their own lives in a world inhospitable to goodness. It is no accident that some of the best-known misanthropes – Zhuangzi, Montaigne, the mature Rousseau, for example – were men who had 'seen it all' and retired into relative seclusion from the world of affairs, acutely aware of the limits on how they, or anyone else, could influence the course of things. They might be described as quietists.

It is important to appreciate that quietism is not shoulder-shrugging indifference. It is precisely because they are disturbed and depressed by the truth of the misanthropic verdict that quietists seek to shape their lives in ways that respond to this verdict. Nor does quietism entail the abandonment of action – of, for example, action that alleviates the suffering of some creatures. But it does mean maintaining a focus on what one can sensibly hope to achieve oneself, rather than on the prospects of big 'causes' and social movements. The poet and farmer, Wendell

Berry, expresses the point well, when criticising 'that will-o'-the-wisp, the large-scale solution to the large-scale problem'. This is because it 'serves mostly to distract people from the small, private problems that they may . . . have the competence to solve'.[17] The quietist wants to live in accordance with the virtues, to become as free from failings and vices as he or she can reasonably and realistically aspire to be. It is no objection – indeed, is irrelevant – to this desire that other people remain entangled in forms of life that encourage these failings and vices. The quietist has no illusions about changing how the rest of the world lives, but will at least be able to say, as does one activist, 'I realise that animals will continue to suffer and die – but not because of me'.[18]

The quietist may literally withdraw from the world. It is out of misanthropy, of 'disillusionment with the world', a theatre of suffering, that many Buddhist forest monks are described as 'withdrawing from the world' in order to keep themselves 'unspotted'.[19] But when Zhuangzi, having warned us not to 'labour . . . over aspects of life [we] can do nothing about', advises us to 'let go of the world' and become 'free of entanglements', he is not urging us to become hermits.[20] The detachment or distance from the world that he recommends is one of the spirit, a disentanglement from various attitudes – and from the practices they inform – that breed and nourish failings and vices characteristic of modern life.

There are four related attitudes or 'mindsets' in particular from which you or I should try to detach and distance ourselves if, so the quietist argues, our lives are to be proper responses to the truth of misanthropy. They are attitudes that, to the detriment of the good life, pervade the practices, policies and institutions of modern societies. I'll name them scientism, technologism, humanism and perfectionism. Scientism is the conviction that only the natural sciences provide genuine understanding and knowledge of the world and of life. Technologism is the assumption that applied science – the enterprise of technology – is the primary or even the sole means to the achievement of human goals. Humanism, encapsulated in the slogan 'man is the measure', is the doctrine that what is valuable is so only in relation to the goals that human beings set themselves. Perfectionism – Rousseau's ironically named 'faculty of self-improvement' (see p. 33 above) – is a restless concern with esteem that drives demands for 'progress', especially in the sphere of material well-being, and a corresponding inability to remain still and content with what one is and has.

These four 'isms' come as a package, with each of them serving to reinforce the rest. Thus, the scientistic outlook encourages the dismissal, as 'sentimental', of moral qualms about practices that deliver human goals, thereby clearing the way for technological interventions – experiments on animals, say – that in turn stimulate hopes and demands for further progress. Or the dynamic might be like this: a perfectionist demand (for the production and availability of ever cheaper meat, perhaps) is translated by the humanist into a moral 'right' that technology is then mobilised to deliver, thereby enhancing the prestige of the sciences that make possible these technical feats (the genetic engineering of pigs, say).

Together, the four 'isms' are woven into societies dedicated to complex and sophisticated enterprises, like that of industrialised agriculture. Together, they define a form of life marked by the frenzy and busy-ness on which I've remarked more than once. In contrast with 'savage man', wrote Rousseau, 'civilised man' is 'over-busy. . . [and] sweats, scurries about and constantly frets in search of ever more . . . occupations' and goals.[21] Already, in fourth-century BCE China, the Daoist sages observed that, with the atrophy of the sense of a guiding Way and with the availability of new and clever technologies, everyone felt the need for 'something to do', 'scurrying about even when sitting still' in febrile attempts to achieve their ever-changing goals and aspirations.[22]

Busy-ness characterises a form of life that is hospitable to the failings and vices emphasised earlier in connection, especially, with our treatment of animals. Greed, for example, that is constantly renewed and redirected by the enticing prospects opened up by technological progress. Or a collective hubris – an image of ourselves as 'lords of the earth' – that is implicit both in the conceit of scientism and in the humanist elevation of humankind to being the sole measure of value and meaning. Or the kind of toxic mindlessness that stands in the way of seeing things for what they are, instead of through the distorting lens of their use and place in the furtherance of human ambitions.

The attitudes from which the quietist seeks detachment and distance, entrenched as they are in modern human life, are not universal or inevitable. There have been cultures in which the idea that truth and understanding is the preserve of the natural sciences would have seemed laughable. There have been cultures, too, in which peaceful and modest acceptance of our limitations, instead of a Promethean perfectionism, has prevailed. More relevantly, it is open to an individual person living in societies defined by these attitudes to resist them, to hold them at a distance. It would, in fact, be a form of bad faith to maintain that each person is a helpless victim of the 'isms'.

I spoke of the quietist's detachment from a world penetrated by these attitudes as one of the spirit, rather than, necessarily, the literal detachment of a hermit or forest monk. But I don't mean that this detachment must be 'inner', a matter simply of thought and feeling without connection to bodily and worldly engagement. Precisely because the four 'isms' pervade everyday practice, resistance to them must express itself in ways of acting and living, ways out of tune with the prevailing attitudes. Detachment is not an operation that takes place in the confines of the soul, but is enacted in a person's relationship to other people, to him- or herself, and to animals and nature.

In fact, one sees everywhere – even or especially in the urban heartland of cultures in which the 'isms' prevail – people manifesting, in lots of little ways, resistance and detachment. Slow food, yoga, urban gardening, meditation, retreats, 'greening' . . . in these and many other ways, people accommodate to, but without surrendering to, a world that they perceive as productive of failings and vices destructive of the good life. And many of these people do so without illusions, innocent of any pretence that their modest practices of detachment will bring about a new world.

Animals have been recessive in this chapter. It has been concerned with various general ways of responding to misanthropy, ranging from rejection to radical confrontation to quietist accommodation. This last response, quietism, was understood in terms of a movement of detachment and distance from attitudes and practices characteristic of contemporary human life. But, as some of the examples given of ways in which people make this movement suggest, it is a movement not only of detachment, but at the same time of convergence. The urban gardener, for instance, seeks distance from the entanglements of modern life, but through cultivating intimacy with natural, living things. For anyone whose recognition of the truth of misanthropy is motivated by reflections, like the ones in this book, on animals and our relationship with them, one form of convergence will be especially significant. This, of course, is convergence with the lives of animals – the topic to which I now turn.

NOTES

1 Giacomo Leopardi, *Thoughts*, London: Hesperus, 2002, p. 85.
2 See Andrew Gibson, *Misanthropy: The Critique of Humanity*, London: Bloomsbury, 2017, p. 2.
3 Quoted in Gibson, *Misanthropy*, p. 14.

4 Schopenhauer, *The World as Will and Representation*, Vol. I, New York: Dover, p. 393.

5 For this point, see Alain de Botton, in *Do Humankind's Best Days Lie Ahead?: Munk Debate 2015*, London: OneWorld, 2016, pp. 12, 72.

6 Steven Pinker, *The Better Angels of our Nature*, London: Penguin, 2011, p. 795.

7 Ibid. pp. 672, 688, 841.

8 Ibid. p. 791.

9 Ibid. p. 712.

10 Ibid. p. 570.

11 Ibid. p. 573.

12 Leopardi, *Thoughts*, p. 44; *The Moral Essays*, New York: Columbia University Press, 1983, pp. 65, 219.

13 On Hartmann, see Frederick C. Beiser, *Weltschmerz: Pessimism in German Philosophy 1860–1900*, Oxford: Oxford University Press, 2016, Chapter 7.

14 Ludwig Wittgenstein, *Culture and Value*, Oxford: Blackwell, 1980, p. 56.

15 Wendell Berry, *What Are People For?* San Francisco, CA: North Point, 1990, p. 201.

16 Melanie Joy, *Why We Love Dogs, Eat Pigs, and Wear Cows*, San Francisco, CA: Red Wheel Weiser, 2010, pp. 133–4.

17 Berry, *What Are People For?* p. 198.

18 Quoted in Joy, *Why We Love Dogs . . .* , p. 143.

19 Michael Carrithers, *The Forest Monks of Sri Lanka*, Oxford: Oxford University Press, 1983, pp. 9, 23.

20 Brook Ziporyn (tr.), *Zhuangzi: The Essential Writings*, Indianapolis, IN: Hackett, 2009, p. 77.

21 Jean-Jacques Rousseau, *Discourse on the Origin of Inequality*, Oxford: Oxford University Press, 1994, p. 83.

22 Hans-Georg Moeller (tr.), *Daodejing: A Complete Translation and Commentary*, Chicago: Open Court, 2007, Chapter 20; Ziporyn, *Zhuangzi*, p. 27.

9

BEING WITH ANIMALS

Misanthropy in the sense discussed in this book is motivated, in significant part, by reflection on our relationships with animals. An important dimension of the question of a person's accommodation to the truth of misanthropy will therefore revolve around attitudes and comportment towards animals. What is an appropriate way – one conducive to living well – of relating to animals? I begin by considering an approach to such questions that is prominent in modern moral theory but, in my view, deflects from addressing them properly. I then develop a less theoretically charged approach in terms of ways of being with animals.

RATIONALITY

Many contemporary philosophers propose that the main requirement for treating animals well is the exercise of reason. For what reason delivers, they argue, is recognition of the moral status and moral rights of animals. A correct relation to animals, consequently, is respect for this status and these rights. What makes it rational to recognise animal rights is, supposedly, the illogicality of confining moral rights to human beings. This is no more rational than confining them to, say, young people or members of a particular race. Hence the term 'speciesism', coined on the model of 'ageism', 'racism' and 'sexism', to name and shame those guilty of irrational discrimination against animals. In each case, moral regard is being refused beings that, in all morally relevant respects (like sensitivity to pain), are similar to ones within the circle of moral regard. Expansion of this circle – from an original regard only for, say, one's fellow tribesmen – has been a process of reason, and further expansion of it to include non-human animals is a continuation of this process.[1] The convergence of humans with animals that matters, then, is shared occupation of this circle, the realm of beings with moral status and rights. This is a convergence dictated solely by reason; rational regard for their status and rights, not emotions like compassion, defines a morally acceptable relationship to animals.

I won't dwell at length on the deficiencies of this approach.[2] Most of these stem from the high level of abstraction of the approach. In every culture, the status and respect accorded to different animals is contextually grounded. A people's totem animal, for example, is honoured by them in a manner that other creatures are not. Pets can rightfully expect care from their owners that other animals cannot.[3] But the status and rights that the moral theorist speaks of are ones possessed by animals in general, irrespective of their actual place in any culture. This makes it difficult to understand the force and very meaning of the respect and regard the theorist calls for. In talking of respect for all animals, rather than for those to which people have certain relations, the term is drained of the sense it has in real life contexts.

It is also hard to see what explanatory role these abstract rights are supposed to have. The status accorded a totem animal explains why animals of that kind are, for example, buried with honour, but the moral status we are urged to accord all animals plays no role in how we treat any of them. In the example of the unfortunate turkey (p. 91 above), it was not ignorance of the equal rights of humans and birds, but 'stone-heartedness', of which its killers were guilty.

Abstraction is responsible, too, for the idleness of the approach – its failure to yield practical guidance. 'All animals have rights', it is proclaimed – but then what? Does it mean, for instance, that animals should not be killed for food? There are good reasons to be vegetarian, but they don't include the blanket assertion that animals have rights. If, having heard the reasons, you conclude that animals have a right not be eaten by us, this will be the outcome, not the premise, of the case against meat-eating. The idea of rights will have played no part in the case. If turkeys are to avoid the fate of the one just mentioned, this will be due, not to the dawning of a philosophical truth about rights, but to compassion and the atrophy of a perception of the birds as walking meat.

An emphasis on rationality is found not only among philosophers who urge the expansion of a moral circle to include animals, but in books that powerfully document our crimes against animals. As suggested by the titles of some of these – *Why We Love Dogs, Eat Pigs, and Wear Cows* or *Some We Love, Some We Hate, Some We Eat* – the focus is on the striking contrasts, both within and across cultures, in how animals are regarded and treated. Puppies pampered in Germany are on the menu in Korean restaurants. In an English garden, people feed robins and tits, then go out on the nearby moors to massacre other birds. But when the authors refer to the 'inconsistencies and paradoxes', the 'gaping holes in logic' and 'contradictions' evidenced by these differences, it is clear they want to highlight, not just contrasts, but the alleged irrationality of our practices.[4]

Inadvertently or not, this emphasis on irrationality encourages the idea that the fundamental wrong in our ways of regarding and treating animals is their inconsistency. We stand accused, primarily, not of cruelty, indifference, hubris and other vices, but of unreason. This serves to deflect the attention, demanded by the misanthrope, on a wide range of entrenched vices and failings. It serves, too, to 'let us off the hook', or at any rate to soften the force of the misanthropic verdict. For most of us would prefer cheerfully to own up to inconsistencies than to admit to vanity, callousness, wilful ignorance and self-serving illusions. Better to concede gaping holes in one's logic than moral failings in one's character.

Is it anyway true that practices towards animals are shot through with contradictions? Contrasts between ways animals are treated are not necessarily contradictions, and stark differences in attitudes to them need not be paradoxical. Irrationality is not, in fact, the right kind of charge to make against Koreans who keep some dogs as pets and eat others, or against Englishmen who feed some birds and shoot others. This isn't because these practices are, after all, impeccably rational, playing their allotted part within some logically coherent cultural whole. Like most cultural practices and attitudes, they are neither demanded by nor forbidden by reason: they simply emerge and grow up as part of the great motley that constitutes a society's form of life. Traditions, including the eating of dogs and shooting birds for entertainment, coexist alongside countless others, including keeping pet dogs and feeding garden birds. That people who inherit these contrasting traditions could not provide them with a rationale does not mean they are illogical. Traditions are not the work of planners and social engineers, whether logical or illogical. They are simply there, currents in the flow of cultural life.

It's possible, no doubt, to find genuine contradictions, witting or otherwise, in what people say or between this and their actions, and those who chronicle attitudes to animals are right to expose them. But susceptibility to such inconsistencies is, for the misanthrope, low on the charge list of the failings and vices responsible for our treatment of animals. It won't therefore be, solely or mainly, through corrections to our reasoning that convergence with animals is cultivated.

ATTUNEMENT

What motivates theories of the moral status and rights of animals is a perceived need to explain what is wrong with, say, the cruelties of bear-baiting or rhino poaching. These are wrong, the explanation goes, because they violate the rights of animals.

But this is a peculiarly dog-legged way of identifying the wrongs done. Once it is recognised that suffering is being inflicted on animals out of greed or for entertainment, no further explanation is required of why these are wrongs. The misanthrope in Chapter 6 was right to say that, in a sense, it's just obvious what's wrong with our usage of animals – it is the product or expression of our vices and failings. We are 'party to a huge amount of animal suffering which could be substantially reduced if we changed. . . . Therefore, most of us should change'.[5] The inference here is immediate, and there is no reason to lubricate it by putting in a mention of violated rights. What we should look for, therefore, by way of a response to the misanthropic verdict, is not commitment to some moral theory but awareness of what we do to animals and of the failings this manifests.

This is an awareness, of course, that crucially involves mindfulness of the animals themselves. Though she is a critic of the rhetoric of rights, the philosopher and animal trainer Vicki Hearne, whom we encountered in Chapter 3, proposes that animals do, however, have one 'unalienable' right – a right to 'be believed in'.[6] By this she at least means that we should recognise animals as beings with perspectives and purposes of their own, as subjects of lives that matter to them, as participants in worlds of significance. This is to recognise, in effect, the truths about animal lives articulated in Chapter 3. But to recognise this only in the manner of a detached scientist or philosopher is not what Hearne has in mind. The being of a dog is not simply there to understand, but to 'listen to'.[7] Indeed, 'understanding' is not always the right word for what is gained from listening. Hearne's own dog, Joe, like all animals, has an opacity; she cannot always 'penetrate [his] otherness' so as, for example, to 'share [his] vision' of an exercise she has taught him.[8]

To listen properly is to become attuned, so let's speak of culti-vating an attunement to animals as a way of relating to animals that we should aspire to. Since someone who is attuned to some-thing becomes closer to, more familiar and intimate with it, attunement to animals is a form of convergence with them – the kind required in an accommodation to the truth of misanthropy. The question is how to foster this attunement, one that makes it unthinkable to carry on as usual with the kinds of treatment of animals exposed by the misanthrope.

Part of the answer was indicated in the previous chapter – resistance to attitudes or mindsets, such as technologism, that occlude or distort people's perception of animals, and indeed of everything else. As some of the examples I gave suggested, attunement to animals will play a significant part in this resis-tance. For resistance, we saw, is not some 'inner' spiritual feat. To resist the grip of humanism, scientism and technologism is, necessarily, to conduct one's life in some ways rather than others. Equally, attunement to animals must manifest itself in our lives, in our practices – ones that, in their turn, will shape and refine the attunement they express. Let's call the motley of these prac-tices of attunement 'being with animals'.

It goes without saying that being with animals is not sim-ply a matter of spending a lot of time among animals. Abattoir workers do that, as do scientists who test dogs' experience of pain and people who extract bile from bears. Theirs are practices that require no recognition of – no listening to – the perspec-tives, aims and goods of the animals with which they deal. For them, attunement to the animals is redundant, and may even be an obstacle. It can't, for example, help the budding laboratory researcher to dwell on the fact that the cringing dog in the cage once had a home, an environment that mattered to it and in which it led a meaningful life.

So what ways of being with animals are apt for cultivating attunement? In many religious and spiritual traditions, there is nostalgia for a time – a golden age – in which human beings and animals lived together in harmony and friendship. Daoists, for example, imagine an age – one of 'perfect virtue' – when 'the birds and beasts clustered together with each other. . . [and] the people lived together with the birds and beasts'. People then knew 'the habits of all the myriad things' and could 'interpret' – listen to – their 'sounds and gestures'.[9]

Buddhists, too, imagine such an era and, still in recent times and in some places, attempt to coexist with animals in ways that recall the virtues of that lost or mythical time. In a charming and perceptive portrait of life in a Sri Lankan village during the early part of the twentieth century, the author recounts how 'we are good friends with the fish', unlike the 'coast dwellers'. who 'lack all feeling' and for whom fishing is an 'industry or sport'. While it is right to put a premium on protecting human beings, it is 'sinful' unnecessarily to destroy the nests of cobras and ants. The lives of the villagers' cattle are interwoven with their own: they have 'helped the evolution' of the cattle just as, in turn, the cattle have 'furthered [their] own moral susceptibilities'. When the great bull, Nakiya ('Old Man'), dies he is buried with dignity, not out of sentimentality, but out of a sense that the village had been 'privileged' by him and that he should always be 'part of our land'.[10] Buddhist monks, too, often give voice to the perception that 'animals are our friends' and that it should be everyday practice to help those that need it – orphaned squirrels, say, or even tadpoles.[11] The precedent is set by the Buddha himself, who is often portrayed as being with animals – with, for example, an elephant that, like himself, sometimes wants respite from the crowd or the herd. Countless haikus of the 'Pure Land' Buddhist poet, Issa – whose 'neighbours' were 'boars and bears' – describe how butterflies, sparrows, frogs, cats and dogs should be welcomed to participate in festivals and rituals as well as in everyday human life.[12]

Expressed in these traditions is an ideal of being with animals where human and animal lives are closely interwoven and inflect one another. Their worlds and our worlds are, in Jakob von Uexküll's memorable image, 'countless environments' that merge and modulate in a 'symphony of meaning'.[13] The golden age of living together with the birds and beasts is, of course, a myth, and in the contemporary world few people have the desire or opportunity to belong to simple communities in which men, women and children dwell in peace and friendship alongside animals. But even in our modern world, there are little ways in which individual people may let animals into their lives and be attuned to them.

Most obviously, they can have pets, companion animals. Pets, we know, suffer brutality and indignity at the hands of many owners, but at its best the relationship between a human being and a companion animal is one of beauty and goodness. A pet dog offers an opportunity to listen to an animal's being, to experience the presence of a creature that leads a life that matters to it. Thomas Mann, in a biographical tribute to his pointer, Bashan, eloquently describes the 'ambiguous' character of the relationship. Because their two lives intersect so closely, it is one in which he is 'intimate' with Bashan's pleasures and concerns, in which aspects of the dog's being are 'revealed' and salient. But it is also a relationship with a creature whose nature is 'alien', 'strange', 'inscrutable'. To be attuned to a dog's being is to combine understanding or insight with appreciation of its opacity, recognition that the dog himself is, as Mann puts it, also attuned to 'other orders' of being than our own.[14]

If having pets can be a way of being with animals, so can having a garden. Like the Chinese sage, Liezi, we may invite birds and animals into our gardens and be happy when they feel as much at home there as they do in their usual habitats. To welcome the returning swallows to the garden shed in the spring, or simply to watch sparrows and goldfinches feeding at the table in the winter, is once again to experience intersections of human and animal lives. If the birds depend on the garden, the gardeners equally depend on the birds for appreciating the rhythm of the seasons, the tempos of nature and the integral place in the natural order of, not only the birds, but of all animals.

There are many ways besides keeping pets and hospitality to wildlife in the garden in which even urban dwellers living in a highly technological society may cultivate attunement to animals. Wildlife photography, for example, or simply mindful walking through parks, along towpaths, or in the surrounding woods and fields. One product of these practices is liable to be an enhanced appreciation of the beauty of animals. Enjoyment of their beauty is not hived off from understanding the animals and their virtues. The beauty of the stag we see on the hill is not detachable from the dignity and courage that we also perceive in the creature. We experience a dog running on the beach as beautiful in part because it is expressive of a capacity for joy, a zest for living. The beauty of a falcon 'loosed in the warm spring sky', wrote J.A. Baker, is a symbol of what 'freedom means'.[15]

If hands-on, practical engagement with animals is impossible for a person, there are still available 'virtual' or vicarious forms of acquaintance with them. The most obvious and easily available are television programmes. Almost every night on the main channels alone there are likely to be half a dozen programmes devoted to animals – to wildlife, patients in a veterinary practice, the antics of pets, or whatever. Some of these are guilty, with their sentimentality and sensationalism, of distorting the natures of the creatures whose lives they are supposedly presenting, but at their best, animal programmes can inform, show, make vivid and provide a sense of how animals are and how some people succeed in sharing their lives with them. It's possible indirectly to foster attunement to animals by watching and listening to people who are more directly attuned. The same is true of reading about animals – not just books on zoology and animal ethology, but more 'personal', even fictional, ones that describe their authors' relationships with the animals they know. For example, there are the books we've already encountered that convey insight into human–dog relations – Thomas Mann's *Bashan and I*, J. R. Ackerley's *My Dog Tulip*, Milan Kundera's *The Unbearable Lightness of Being* or Monty Don's *Nigel*.

One thing that films or books do is acquaint us with men and women who are exemplars of good ways of being with animals. These are people who we feel to be properly attuned to the animals they engage with, hence people to emulate. The Buddha, St Francis of Assisi, the biologist Konrad Lorenz, the primatologist Jane Goodall, the veterinarian Noel Fitzpatrick . . . these are just a handful of the figures who emphatically strike us as attuned to the animals they encounter, nourish, study or cure. In all areas of the moral life, exemplars have a powerful role.[16] In such people, we encounter living embodiments of virtues to which otherwise we might merely nod our approval; they help to give us a sense for how it is to live in a manner informed by these virtues – and hence serve as models for us to emulate. So, a good way vicariously to seek attunement to animals is by acquainting ourselves with exemplars – heroes, as it were – of attunement.

This has been a brief and partial sketch of ways through which to be with animals, to cultivate attunement to them. I haven't, for example, mentioned the opportunities many of us have to help with the care of animals – walking trainee guide dogs, for example, or working a few hours a week in a rescue home. But it's time to turn to the question of how this attunement contributes to a life freer from failings and vices than the kind the misanthrope has been describing.

VIRTUES, EMULATION AND MYSTERY

How, the question is, may attunement and being with animals cultivate a way of living that responds to the truth of the misanthropic verdict? The answer, unsurprisingly, is that they do so by fostering certain virtues. And they do so, I suggest, in three ways – by militating against various failings, inspiring emulation of animals and inviting a sense of the mystery of things.

We know that people whose work is with animals – in the abattoir, the laboratory, the factory farm and elsewhere – often treat them callously. But we know, as well, that many of them need to overcome a reluctance to engage in such work – something they manage to do under pressure to earn a wage or advance a career, or just through getting used to the work. The ways of being with animals I sketched earlier are not jobs; they're not engaged in to make a living or in response to pressing needs and ambitions. They are ways, accordingly, through which compassion and related virtues – for example, the 'sympathetic joy' at the flourishing of a creature, of which Buddhists speak – are apt to find lasting expression. The woman who feeds birds in her garden will care about them when an icy winter threatens, and then rejoice in the appearance of fledglings at the table a few months later.

Being with animals also militates against the willed ignorance and indifference that are among the failings most obviously responsible for crimes against animals. The person attuned to animals through being with them is, by definition, attentive to their nature and needs, 'listening to' their being, and someone for whom they have significance. Being with them, even indirectly and vicariously, is to close that distance between human and animal lives that permits indifference and ignorance.[17]

People attuned to animal lives cannot pretend to know nothing about what it is like for creatures to endure confinement and worse. And it requires a peculiar psychology for the care they exercise towards the animals that they understand not to extend at all to animals more generally. Attunement to animals is convergence with animal life at large.

It is not only by directly engaging virtues, like compassion and mindfulness, that being with animals promotes the virtues. It does so, too, by inspiring emulation of aspects of animal lives. Some earlier remarks in this chapter prepare for this point. The beauty of animals, I argued, may symbolise or evoke qualities that we admire, and certain people, I noted, are exemplars whom we are drawn to emulate. My present point is that not only people, but animals too can exemplify virtues and – not least through the beauty with which they do so – draw us to emulate them.

Emulation does not of course mean becoming a 'furry', dressing up as an animal, barking or miaowing, devouring roadkill and the like. It is not an attempt, like that of the central figure in Han Kang's novel *The Vegetarian*, to 'shuck off the human'.[18] Nor does it mean adopting the lifestyle of Tarzan, Mowgli or other figures brought up by and among animals. Emulation is seeking to translate into an authentically human life virtues that are especially salient in the lives of some animals – virtues that might otherwise have less prominence for us than they should. It's often proposed, for instance, that a dog provides a model of an 'unconditional love' that remains admirably immune to judgements about the person who is loved. The example, though, is controversial; what some praise as unconditional and non-judgemental, others denounce as blind.

It is to a different, less controversial animal virtue I want to turn – spontaneity. A fundamental aspect of human existence, we saw in Chapter 3, was a sense of a self indefinitely extended in time, with all this implies by way of concern for past and future states of one's self. This dimension of human being is a precondition for human achievements, but also for vanity, greed and other failings listed in Chapter 4. It is a precondition, too, of an incapacity to enjoy the moment, indeed to appreciate anything except in relation to self-imposed strategies that, we hope, will enable us to achieve the goals we constantly feel compelled to set ourselves. Spontaneity is the antithesis of this incapacity; a flexible, responsive attention to things as they are, an appreciation of the moment irrespective of its connection with some future goal. It is a virtue because it liberates a person, if only temporarily, from the grip of purposiveness, from entanglement in schemes, plans and the busy-ness of life in complex technological societies.

What invites admiration of dogs, writes Jeffrey Masson, 'harks back to a time when humans were more like dogs, more spontaneous . . . able to enjoy the world outside our skins more immediately'.[19] It is this spontaneity that Mark Rowlands admired in his pet wolf, Brenin. Whereas we seem compelled to engage in a febrile pursuit of 'what is new and different', each moment of Brenin's life is 'complete'; happiness, for him, is 'the eternal return of the same'.[20] The words of both authors recall a famous poem by Rilke in which he writes of the animal 'look[ing] into the Open', at 'what exists . . . without regard for who he is', and thereby enjoying an 'indescribably open freedom'. The animal's world is 'unsupervised' and 'unformulated'.[21] This is a world experience which is not regimented and constrained by the self-concerns, preconceptions, worries and ambitions that stand between human beings and reality.

Spontaneity is freedom from *idées fixes*, rigid categories of thought, prejudices, self-serving illusions and much else characteristic of the human condition. Spontaneity (*ziran*, literally 'self-so-ness') was the paramount Daoist virtue; the spontaneous person, in fact, emulates the *dao* itself since 'the *dao* follows the way of spontaneity', a way free from distortion, constraint and purpose.[22] It is no surprise to find, in the Daoist classics, admiration, fondness and sympathy for animals, and nostalgia for an age when our lives converged more closely with theirs. To attune ourselves to animals, to be with them, and to emulate their spontaneity is a way in which a person might recall and retrieve a virtue of that lost age.

Finally, being with animals invites a sense of the mystery of things. On several occasions, I've referred to the opacity of animals, and many authors I've mentioned – J.M. Coetzee, Vicki Hearne and Thomas Mann, for example – are impressed by what the last of these called the 'ambiguity' of animals, their transparency in some respects, their opacity or mystery in others. And most of us, I suggest, when we are mindfully in the company of animals are struck by the mystery of their existence. This mystery, I argued in Chapter 3, is not due to our inability to penetrate the 'inner' recesses of a dog's or cat's mind. That, after all, is something we can't do in the case of our fellow human beings either. Rather, it is the impossibility of fully imagining the canine, feline and other animal worlds, of knowing how the world figures and shows up for an animal, how the world is organised for it, what stands out for it as significant and what is just background 'noise'. The worlds that cats experience, like those that we do, are spheres of significance in which things figure and have meaning in relation to the lives they lead. Animal worlds intersect with ours, but they do not coincide, and what its world as a whole is like for an animal is something we cannot know.

So there is mystery here. But how could of this be part of an accommodation to misanthropy? How might attunement to the mystery of animals contribute to a person's resistance to the failings and vices the misanthrope identifies? Important to recall, here, is that these failings and vices include, or are rooted in, various mindsets and attitudes – among them, collective hubris and the pretensions of humanism, scientism and technologism discussed in Chapter 8. Now, recognition of the mystery of animals is itself a summons to modesty, a challenge to hubristic claims, by champions of humanism and scientism, of the limitless reach of human knowledge. More vital, however, is to reflect on how the mystery of animals enables appreciation of a wider mystery – that of the very emergence of worlds for us and other beings to experience at all.

No one can seriously doubt that a dog experiences a world and that this world is different from any human world of experience. It makes no sense, in my view, to ask which of countless worlds of experience – the dog's, mine, an ancient hunter-gatherer's, an elephant's, an angel's, a dalek's – corresponds to reality as such, to how things are independently of the perspectives and purposes of the creatures that experience and engage with them. To suppose, as we typically do, that the human perspective is uniquely privileged is pure hubris. As Nietzsche remarked, it is no less hubristic than the 'solemnity' with which a gnat might proclaim its unique access to truth.[23] It is no use replying that, unlike gnats, we have developed the sciences; for the sciences are no less founded on and shaped by peculiarly human concerns, goals and perspectives than the arts and everything else we engage in.[24]

Now if no world of experience is privileged, it must be a mystery how these worlds emerge, how experience – human or animal – is possible. It cannot be explained by turning to the sciences or to theology, since these are pervaded by partial, 'all-too-human' perspectives. You can't explain the emergence of a whole world of experience by a parochial appeal to perspectives of just the kind you are supposed to be explaining.

Just how much of our crimes against animals – and, indeed, against people and the planet – can be put down to collective hubris and anthropocentric pretensions is hard to gauge. But more obvious moral failings responsible for these crimes, like vanity and greed, are surely helped to prosper by an ideology, a context of thought and value, in which human goals and forms of understanding are taken to dictate how things are and should be. It is by way of response to such an ideology that, to recall Carl Safina's moving words, people should join with the animals in a common quest to 'live out the mystery and opportunity of finding ourselves somehow in existence'.

To participate in this quest is as good a way as we can sensibly hope for, perhaps, by way of accommodation to the misanthropic verdict – of finding a prospect of happiness despite recognising what a great poet, alert to mystery of animals, called 'the dreadfulness of life'.[25] To provide a reminder of the prospect of this participation is as good a way as any, perhaps, to end a book that, by reflecting on our relations with animals, has defended that verdict.

NOTES

1 On the expanding moral circle and 'speciesism', see Peter Singer, *The Expanding Circle: Ethics and Sociobiology*, Princeton, NJ: Princeton University Press, 2011.

2 For a more detailed criticism, see David E. Cooper, 'Animals, Attitudes and Moral Theories', in I. J. Kidd and L. McKinnell (eds.), *Science and the Self: Animals, Evolution and Ethics: Essays in Honour of Mary Midgley*, London: Routledge, 2015, pp. 19–30. See also the criticisms of moral status theories in Rosalind Hursthouse, *Ethics, Humans and Other Animals*, London: Routledge, 2000, and Tzachi Zamir, *Ethics and the Beast*, Princeton, NJ: Princeton University Press, 2007.

3 On the cultural and contextual variety in people's relations to different animals, see the classic study by James Serpell, *In the Company of Animals: A Study of Human-Animal Relationships*, Oxford: Blackwell, 1986.

4 See Melanie Joy, *Why We Love Dogs, Eat Pigs, and Wear Cows*, San Francisco, CA: Red Wheel Weiser, 2010, and Hal Herzog, *Some We Love, Some We Hate, Some We Eat: Why Is It So Hard to Think about Animals?* New York: Harper Perennial, 2011, for these and many other references to our alleged unreason.

5 Hursthouse, *Ethics, Humans and Other Animals*, p. 166.

6 Vicki Hearne, *Adam's Task: Calling Animals by Name*, New York: Skyhorse, 2007, p. 266.

7 Ibid. p. 59.

8 Ibid. p. 30.

9 Brook Ziporyn (tr.), *Zhuangzi: The Essential Writings*, Indianapolis, IN: Hackett, 2009, p. 61; A. C. Graham (tr.), *The Book of Lieh-Tzu*, New York: Columbia University Press, 1990, Chapter 2.

10 J. Vijayatunga, *Grass for My Feet*, London: Howard Baker, 1970, pp. 29, 31, 66, 112, 115.

11 Michael Carrithers, *The Forest Monks of Sri Lanka*, Oxford: Oxford University Press, 1983, pp. 284, 291.

12 See J. Ireland (tr.), *The Udāna*, Kandy: Buddhist Publication Society, 1990, 4.5, and David G. Lanoue, *Issa and the Meaning of Animals: A Buddhist Poet's Perspective*, New Orleans: HaikuGuy.com, 2014, passim.

13 Jakob von Uexküll, *A Foray into the Worlds of Animals and Human: With a Theory of Meaning*, Minneapolis: University of Minnesota Press, 2010, p. 208.

14 Thomas Mann, *Bashan and I*, Pittsburgh: University of Pennsylvania Press, 2003, pp. 84, 93.

15 J.A. Baker, *The Peregrine*, New York: New York Review of Books, 2005, p. 178.

16 On exemplars, see Linda Zagzebski, *Exemplarist Moral Theory*, Cambridge: Cambridge University Press, 2017, and Ian James Kidd, 'Spiritual Exemplars', *International Journal of Philosophy and Theology*, forthcoming 2018.

17 Martin Heidegger makes a similar point, to which my discussion owes, about the 'deserving', or distance reducing, character of what he too calls 'being with'. See his *Being and Time*, Oxford: Blackwell, 1980, § 26.

18 Han Kang, *The Vegetarian*, London: Portobello, 2015, p. 179.

19 Jeffrey Masson, *Dogs Never Lie about Love*, London: Vintage, 1997, p. 185.

20 Mark Rowlands, *The Philosopher and the Wolf*, London: Granta, 2008, pp. 213–4.

21 Rainer Maria Rilke, 'The Eighth Duino Elegy' in G. Good (tr.), *Rilke's Late Poetry*, Vancouver: Ronsdale, 2004, pp. 46–7, and a letter of 25/2/1925 quoted in Heidegger, *Poetry, Language, Thought*, New York: Harper & Row, 1971, p. 108.

22 Hans-Georg Moeller (tr.), *Daodejing: A Complete Translation and Commentary*, Chicago: Open Court, 2007, Chapter 25.

23 Friedrich Nietzsche, *Philosophy and Truth: Selections from Nietzsche's Notebooks of the Early 1870s*, Atlantic Highlands, NJ: Humanities, 1979, p. 79.

24 For a more detailed discussion of animals and mystery, see David E. Cooper, *Senses of Mystery: Engaging with Nature and the Meaning of Life*, London: Routledge, 2017.

25 Rainer Maria Rilke, quoted in Michael Tanner, *Wagner*, London: Flamingo, 1997, p. 199.

Index